LUNAR NOTES

Zoot Horn Rollo's Captain Beefheart Experience

LUNAR NOTES

Zoot Horn Rollo's Captain Beefheart Experience

by

Bill Harkleroad

with
Billy James

SAF Publishing Ltd

SAF Publishing Ltd

First published in 1998 / 2000 by SAF Publishing Ltd.
SAF Publishing Ltd.
Unit 7, Shaftesbury Centre,
85 Barlby Road,
London. W10 6BN
ENGLAND

www.saf.mcmail.com

A CIP catalogue record for this book is available from the British Library.

Text copyright © Bill Harkleroad 1998

ISBN 0 946719 21 7

Front cover photograph: Michael Ochs Archives/Venice, CA

Printed in England by Redwood Books, Trowbridge, Wiltshire.

Contents

Acknowledgements

Bill Harkleroad thanks:

Of course the core band members, John French, Jeff Cotton, Mark Boston, Art Tripp, Elliot Ingber, Alex St. Clair, Roy Estrada.

Henry Kaiser, for his knowledge on this subject, and friendship over the years.

Billy James, for puttin' it together, and his up-beat attitude (maybe it was all that rhythm he studied).

The fans who have reinforced that something I was part of, positively impacted their lives.

Billy James thanks (for their contributions to the project):

Jos Schoone, Robert Gray, Justin Sherrill, Carlo Vitale, Theo Tieman, Richard Kunc.

Websites:

Ant-Bee Web Bizarre
http://ourworld.compuserve.com/homepages/antbee/
PO Box 207, Carolina Beach, NC 28428-0207, USA

Home Page Replica
http://www.shiningsilence.com/hpr

Electricity
http://www.cybercomm.nl/~tiotoa/electr.html

PREFACE

In taking on this project my first reaction was... I can't write, but I was then convinced that this could be done in a way that would be interest-ing and informational to someone that cared about the Beefheart band. Specifically the time of 1968 through 1974... my time.

I am under no illusion that this book is about me, people want to know about Don Van Vliet. Keeping this in mind, all I could really do is describe to the best of my ability what happened, what the process was, what it felt like.

I will never forget the anticipation and excitement I felt going to see Captain Beefheart and his Magic Band for the first time. Being too young to drive, I was dropped off in the parking lot of the Antelope Valley fairgrounds Exposition Hall, to experience my first perform-ance of live music. I had been on a stage previously but not on the other side as a listener.

It was a "huge gig" of maybe 300 people. In 1964 the British inva-sion of style had captured only a few of us, but what was on the stage was the most powerful thing I had ever witnessed. These guys had hair, so important to me at that time, and they were dressed mainly in black (Don was completely in black). As the music was comin' at ya' these larger than life men didn't jump around in a showy display, they stood their ground like pirates that could kick your ass at any moment.

The singer/harp player was wearing sun glasses "indoors at night" and adding more visual power he was sitting down in front of the band. It probably took two or three tunes for me to actually start listening and then, Man-O-Man, this solidified me as a blues player for life!

The idea that I would be in this band wasn't even a dream. These were men and puberty was just taking its toll on me.

I want to thank Billy James for his effort. He's the one that had to decipher and put on paper, my endless ramblings into a tapedeck. I probably should have pulled a few punches in my thoughts on some of the people described here. I think life is hard enough without spreading negativity, but I couldn't start censoring myself and keep the feeling of leaning over to a friend and whispering something.

In recent times "Doctor Dark" has laid a big one on me. Just prior to starting this book I lost my father to cancer. In the middle I very suddenly lost my sister to cancer. Most recently, my long time friend and Beefheart cohort Bill Shumow passed away. In the overpowering wake of these losses, it only seems right to lay to rest what was basically my youth, my "Captain Beefheart" experience.

There were a few times when I either wanted to leave the band, or we were talking about the time it would be all over, that Don in his most "on stage" way would say, "You will never get away from this, it will ALWAYS be with you!" You know what... he was right!

Bill Harkleroad, 1998

FOREWORD
by Henry Kaiser

As I read the manuscript of this book I couldn't help wondering if
Zoot Horn Rollo (aka Bill Harkleroad) wasn't being too modest about
the incredible pioneering musical achievements of the Magic Band
members during his tenure in the band. Not to forget the tremendous
impact and influence that Zoot and his fellow players have had on the
evolution of both pop and experimental music since those days. So, let
me step in here for a moment and try to voice some thoughts in those
directions.

I first saw Captain Beefheart and the Magic Band back in 1967 at
the Avalon Ballroom in San Francisco, a little after the *Safe As Milk*
album was released. Before the show started, I remember a big pile of
bumper stickers being given away under the black lights up on the
Avalon balcony. I took a pile of those home. "Abba Zaba" was being
played a lot on the local underground radio in those days and I was really excited about seeing this band for the first time. When they finally
came out to play I was bowled over by the intensity, impact and origi-
nality of their performance. Sure, Don Van Vliet was an impressive
figure with a giant voice and harp sound - chanting out the lyrics to

"Trust Us" he seemed possessed, like some kind of religious prophet of music from another dimension. But what really impressed me was the band! John French's drumming and body language was more dynamic and exciting than Keith Moon of The Who. Alex and Jeff's guitars mixed feedback with bottleneck neck lines like nothing else in pop music at the time. The rhythms referenced back to the swing, complexity and power of the old Mississippi Delta blues that I loved so much. This was a band with a power, intensity and expression beyond anything else in pop music at the time. For the following five years I went to see every Magic Band gig that I could.

While the personnel changed, up until 1973 all of the Magic Bands had this incredible - well - MAGIC! And as each new album came out I listened over and over on headphones to the new sounds and surprises that were on each release.

I remember one show that I went to at Tufts University in the Boston area back in October of 1971. Mississippi Fred McDowell was the opening act - one of his last gigs - and you could hear the direct connection between his Delta blues and the space age blues of the Beefheart band. I recall Bill and Mark playing a thundering "Peon" in that college gymnasium and finally an incredible improvised solo from Elliot Ingber on "Alice in Blunderland" that made the floor fall away below my feet and impelled me to go out and purchase my first guitar, a black Telecaster that I would later modify with a DeArmond pickup to emulate Zoot - a guitar that I still sometimes play today.

At that time I was running a film society at a residence hall on my college campus. After a few months I was hankering to see the Magic band again. I thought that our film society might branch out and do a concert; so I called up Warner Brothers Records and got the number for the Beefheart management and spoke to Bill Shumow. He told me that the band did not plan to be in my area for a while as they were finishing up a new studio album. He said he'd call me. A month or so later he did, saying that the band was stuck in Boston for a week. He then asked if I had a place where they could rehearse? Fortunately a friend's church basement provided the perfect spot and I got to watch the band rehearse (without Don, of course) for several days. I got to hear the whole *Clear Spot* album played live before it was released and several of my old time favorites such as "Veteran's Day Poppy".

Bill kindly answered many of my young, "beginning-to-play the guitar type" questions and passed along some guitar tips that have served me to this day. I also went along to the Jazz Workshop with Don and Mark to see Joe Henderson play. I remember bringing my roommate, Charlie Olchowski, a Beefheart sceptic (who was sick of hearing *Trout Mask Replica* played over and over in our dorm room) to see the band rehearse and watching his instant musical conversion to a total, rabid fan as the band stood around him in front of Artie's drums and played "Big Eyed Beans from Venus" as an instrumental at bone vibrating volume. That was the real thing!

The band and Don told me to come visit them the next summer up in Trinidad, California and I did so. I stayed in touch and I went to see them play many times. In 1973 I went to a gig in LA (I had spoken to Bill a couple of weeks before and planned to see him at the show) but I was completely shattered when the *Blue Jeans and Moonbeams* new and not-so-Magic Band came out on the stage instead of my friends.

Later, I happened to be in England when Mallard was recording their first album and visited their recording session in a barn on a farm. I talked at length with Mark and Bill about the break-up of the band. They seemed glad to get out of a bad situation, but on the other hand they were sad that a musical era had come to an end. Everyone was feeling a mixture of hurt and relief.

I stayed in touch with Don, visiting him from time to time and eventually met John French in 1975 before the original, and still unreleased, *Bat Chain Puller* album was recorded. That was the beginning of my long friendship and many musical collaborations with Mr. French (aka Drumbo).

Back in 1980 I asked French if he would play drums on a track on my second solo album, *Aloha*. He said yes. Knowing that the Captain could be quite paranoid, I mentioned this to Don. He said that was fine; go ahead. After the album came out I sent a copy to Don. He called me up on the phone and SCREAMED: "My drummer, my drums! Send back that painting I gave you! I don't care if I ever said it was OK! I never want to speak with you again." And he hasn't since.

Well anyway, I've been around this Magic Band music for a long time, I know it well and I've met most of the players. I must say that having observed personally and talked to most of the principals that none of the Beefheart albums would have been the same without the specific members who were in those Magic Bands. As much as Don contributed with his fantastic lyrics and "musical sculpting" to the band's efforts to create new sounds, in my view, the main musical creativity and expression came from the players. Don seemed quick to take as much credit as he could (all, as was his way), but I'm pretty sure that much of the magic came from the other musicians.

Even the latter period magic of *Shiny Beast, Doc at the Radar Station* and *Ice Cream for Crow*, owed so very much to the "real magic" of the bands that contained Zoot Horn Rollo and/or Drumbo. Twice I've had the job of going through the unreleased Beefheart material in the Warner Brothers Records vault. The first time to evaluate things for possible release and the second time to look for material for the *Ice Cream For Crow* band. Many of the songs on Beefheart's last three albums were reconstituted versions of songs originally recorded in the studio or in rehearsal by previous Magic Bands. Sometimes the same titles are used for different songs and it gets confusing. Here then is a handy list to nominate many of those compositions:

From the pre-*Trout Mask Replica* era: "Big Black Baby Shoes" became "Ice Rose", "Dirty Blue Gene" became "The Witch Doctor Life". (These can be heard on the *I May Be Hungry But I Sure Ain't Weird* CD.)

From the *Spotlight Kid* era: "Harry Irene", "Semi-Multicoloured Caucasians", "Drink Paint Run Run" became "Ice Cream for Crow". "Best Batch Yet", "Suzy Murder Wrist" became "Sue Egypt" and "A Carrot is as Close as a Rabbit Gets to a Diamond".

From the *Clear Spot* era: "Dirty Blue Gene", "Little Scratch" became "The Past Sure Is Tense". "Pompadour Swamp" became "Suction Prints".

From the original *Bat Chain Puller* era: "The Thousandth and Tenth Day of the Human Totem Pole", "81 Poop Hatch", "Brick Bats", "The Floppy Boot Stomp", "Flavor Bud Living", "Bat Chain Puller", "Owed T' Alex", "Candle Mambo", "Apes-ma".

This list is only songs that I know for sure to have come from earlier bands since I have heard those earlier recordings myself. Probably several more came from old rehearsal tapes, too.

The influence of the Magic Band members since 1972, both acknowledged and unacknowledged, has been tremendous. Neither European art rock from Henry Cow onwards, or the entire Punk Rock movement, would have been the same without them. From Paul McCartney to Mick Jagger to Kurt Cobain and many more mainstream artists owe inspiration to the Magic Band, and they've all said it in print at one time or another.

For my generation of guitar innovators and improvisers, Zoot Horn Rollo is of paramount importance. I've learned so much from him and have continued to do so over the years. Many of my colleagues such as Eugene Chadbourne, Davey Williams, Jim O'Rourke, Fred Frith, David Torn, Elliott Sharp and Bruce Anderson say likewise. Zoot played things that would have been impossible on guitar. The *Trout Mask Replica* guitar parts are unprecedented. Listen to the complexity and elegance of his playing on *Decals* - it has been surpassed by nothing since. On *Clear Spot* he is an economical rhythm guitar master fusing the stances of American roots artists such as Hubert Sumlin, Fred McDowell, Bukka White and Steve Cropper with a unique slide guitar approach creating something new and different.

On all of the Magic Band and Mallard recordings Bill displays a carefully attained and unique tone and timbre. You can tell with one note or chord that it is him. Look back at any of the albums that Bill is on and you will hear him playing with subtleties of swing, micro-rhythmic feel, and control that is unprecedented in rock music. Most experimental and art rock lacks the grounding in American roots that the best Magic Band music exemplifies. Bill is an innovative and adventurous pioneer who staked out unknown territory and created many beautiful works.

I've always thought it a disservice to the music that the Magic Band members never got their fair share of the credit and were so seldom written about by critics who completely bought Don's version of the genesis of this music. What's been in print up to now has not been consistent with the realities that I have observed and researched. I'm pleased that Zoot's story of the music is finally available here and I hope that it will help others to access and understand this rich musical tradition.

Henry Kaiser

California-based musician Henry Kaiser is widely recognised as one of the most creative and innovative guitarists, improvisers, and producers in the fields of rock, jazz and experimental music. He is also one of the most extensively recorded, having appeared on more than 150 different albums.

CHAPTER ONE
From A Skinny, Pimple-Faced Geek

The first time a trout crossed my musical path was when I snuck out to the garage to listen to this little 45 turntable I had - I don't think it was even equipped to play 33s. I'd saved up my 20 cents or whatever it was to buy an Elvis EP and I danced around in the dark like some fool. I had unplugged the freezer to listen to it, accidentally thawing my dad's prized fish in the process - it was a 26 inch, 5½lb trout that he'd caught.

Appropriately enough my first musical influence was Elvis Presley - I was born on Elvis's 14th birthday, January 8th, 1949. My sister was five years older than me so by the mid-fifties she was well into Presley. It was my first introduction to doo-wop and rockabilly. The whole thing was almost cartoon-like to a 5 or 6 year old like me.

I was born in Long Beach, CA, and lived with my family in Hawthorne, CA. As well as an older sister, I had a brother who was six years younger than me. My dad worked for Douglas and North American Aviation companies building airplanes. My mom was the typical mom - she stayed home.

One day, these two gangster-looking guys - who knows they could have been little nerds selling scotch tape for all I knew - came to the door selling accordion lessons. My mother played, my dad played a little and my sister did too - so my mom turned around and looked back at me and said, "You should take some accordion lessons". I totally freaked out. I hid in the hallway, but I was too afraid to say "No" - so I became an accordion student. I think I made it through one or two lessons and both times I was about ready to cry. But I remember my sister helping me out and I got used to jamming on the thing. I wouldn't so much learn their little tunes but figure out ways to embellish them.

I was 13 in 1962 when I started to play the drums. My best friend at that time was in a band but their drummer never showed up to rehearsals. We played surf music and some Chet Atkins type stuff - very pre-Beatles - it was all totally instrumental music. So I'd sit there and play the standard surf beat. Sometimes I would pick up a guitar and practice the bar chord. My sister had a baritone ukulele and I'd sit out on the corner strumming a bar chord back 'n' forth from A to G à la "Tequila". I thought I was real cool. (Actually it's what I do now with new students, it's a great way to learn).

Anyway I would just sit out there thinking, "I'm cool and the chicks are gonna dig me", all because I'm playing these chords back and forth. I'm sure everybody else thought I was some stupid kid - but I thought I was cool. So, I decided I would become a guitar player. I learned the regular open chords like C, A, D - those real cheapo chords. All of a sudden I'm thinking, "Gee, I'm in a band and I know more than four chords!" After about two weeks rehearsing and learning about 7 or 8 Ventures tunes, I played my first gig as a guitar player and made $7.50. I was on my way and that was that!

I remember borrowing my friend's Silvertone guitar, one of those masonite jobs with the sticky stuff around the edge like contact paper. He lived in this real filthy house and the guitar had peanut butter smeared on the neck. I used to play with this bass player, who instead of playing a bass, played a Fender Jaguar with a 1964 brand new Piggyback Fender bass amp. It was gorgeous, I used to love just smelling it! The other guitarist was also playing a Jaguar and I was playing my borrowed Silvertone. In terms of vocals, I did a few early recordings, mainly at home, but when I heard myself singing on tape I decided it was time, at the tender age of fourteen, to quit singing.

After six or eight months I ended up getting my dad to buy a Fender Duosonic for me. I had to have a Fender. He suggested I get this nice gold Les Paul - a 1954 model - something like that. Of course I thought it was a piece of shit, little did I know. But a Fender's what I wanted. I thought a Duosonic was really *the* one.

So after I got my first guitar we played some parties out at the Littlerock Grange Hall, which was where Frank Zappa had played some early gigs. I later had some tapes of him playing when he was like 19 or 20 and he was a pretty ripping blues guitar player even back then. This was before he switched to drums and started playing for the Blackouts and various other bands in the area.

At highschool I went through various musical stages myself, playing in different bands with all kinds of names like The Polaras, The Nightbeats and The Plague. We played at the local fair and the Battle Of The Bands - at that time it didn't matter so much what you sounded like, if your band had the longest hair you won! Previously I was beaten up in the parking lot for having long hair and being a "faggot". Now, suddenly The Beatles happened and it was, "wait a minute, maybe I am cool after all". It was a great transition for a skinny pimple-faced geek like me!

I never cared much for school. By the last couple years, all I went to were the music classes. I would hang out and smoke pot on the school lawn. The music teacher knew I was kind of a "loady" as I would get high and come in and take flute, saxophone and trumpet classes. It was kinda stupid but that's what I did. Vietnam was raging by then and all I was thinking about was not coming home in a body bag.

Prior to that one of the major moments of my childhood school memory had been the Watts riots. One of my best friends at the time was a black guy named Kenny Freeman who I played a lot of baseball with. Baseball was it for me! I was going to be a big league pitcher.

Kenny was a big influence on me, having turned me on to pot and Jazz - both were equally cool. But when the riots happened there was a complete division between black and white. We were living in an area northeast of LA known as the Antelope Valley (the same area where almost all the early Magic Band members were from). I'll never forget Kenny saying to me, "Well we aren't happenin' right now - maybe sometime in the future". And eventually we did hang out again but that was about six months later, in the meantime a couple of kids from our school were killed. It was something I just couldn't understand.

CHAPTER TWO
Joining The Magic Band

In 1964 Captain Beefheart and the Magic Band were a pretty straight-forward blues band doing Howlin' Wolf, Muddy Waters, Jimmy Reed, John Lee Hooker stuff. They were "the band" in the little town just north of Los Angeles called Lancaster. I too was playing in a local cover band called BC and the Cavemen. In the same band as me was Mark Boston (Rockette Morton), PG Blakely and a singer who was closer in age to the Beefheart band members - they were the "old" guys. They were about 24 which was ancient to a kid of 15.

At that time I used to sit in on a lot of jam sessions. The first time I jammed with the Beefheart band was at a party at Don's house. Don Van Vliet always had "the attitude" but he also had charisma to me - big time charisma - as did the rest of his band but none of them were quite like him. His band consisted of Alex Snouffer (later changed to St. Clair), Doug Moon, Jerry Handley, and former Caveman, PG Blakely. PG has been listed as a piano player, but he was the drummer in both bands.

So anyway, at this particular jam session there were about 30 people crammed into a 15 foot square room. Everyone was smoking pot and drinking. Being 15, I must have been pretty cocky because I was determined to play everything I knew as loud and hard as I could. I obviously turned heads - I could play. These guys had a good feel for old time delta blues and I had been playing BB King licks note-for-note, thanks mainly to Wolfman Jack whose radio show had introduced me to the blues. So I felt real comfortable playing pentatonic blues licks - bending the notes. Like most kids I thought I was real hot because I knew about seven licks.

I could sense I was being noticed and I really wanted to end up in the Magic band - especially as one by one my friends had been asked to join. First however, in the winter of 1967 I joined this group and we all moved to Lake Tahoe to be a "band". I had just graduated from highschool and wasn't doing anything but going to college - mainly just taking acid and smoking as much pot and hash as I could. We rehearsed and played a couple gigs doing Jimi Hendrix covers and a few of our own tunes. We had this guy who had a light show which was a big deal in 1967.

We met up with a crew of people who were Timothy Leary's followers - "the Brotherhood" - a sect of people that were based at Laguna Beach. Their whole deal was this psychedelic prayer book, Alan Watts, and lots of LSD. It was supposed to be this religious based thing, but at my age I was still thinking, "Eh, what's all that about?" - but the drugs were cool! All the time I was just kinda hanging out waiting for the call to join Beefheart's band. I had kept in contact with John French and Jeff Cotton who were both now in his band.

Finally the call came to go down and audition for Don. I hadn't played guitar for a while, probably the only time in my life where I haven't played for over six months - just too stoned! So once I got the call for the audition, I threw my guitar into its case and put 20 joints in my socks and a couple hits of acid in my pocket and got a ride with Jerry Handley, the group's bass player, who was also living in Lancaster. So he drove me down to Woodland Hills for the big try out.

By now all the Beefheart Band, except Jerry, was living together in a house that they had rented on Entrada Drive in Woodland Hills. This was to be my home over the next months and the place where the music for the *Trout Mask Replica* album was conceived. The garden with the bridge, as pictured on the *Trout Mask* LP sleeve, was our back yard. The house itself had two bedrooms, one upstairs that was Don's and a tiny one downstairs that rotated as a room for the rest of us. The living room was the rehearsal space where we could curl up in a corner to sleep. The house had a great garden with all these tropical plants all over the place. In all, there was about an acre of grounds with this funky old house which we thought was bitchin' at the time - but was probably a dump by most people's standards.

Very early on, we played various blues jams, nothing even *Strictly Personal*-ish at all. Don actually sang and played harp - I only found out later how unusual that was. I felt pretty comfortable that they liked what I was playing. After all, I knew all the people I was playing with - Jerry, Jeff, John French and Don. Yet, the vibe was strange - John and Jeff were not the same guys I used to know. They both had a seriously dire look in their eyes, yet on occasions would flip into an almost over-the-top excitement. Jeff was especially animated. So anyway we played these loose blues jams and I just let fly - I hadn't played in a while. The response was, "Oh you're great - you're cool!" and I officially became a member of the Magic Band late June 1968.

After I found out that I was definitely in the band, I remember I went back home and grabbed all my clothes, which was probably about half a suitcase and went right back to the Beefheart house. By the way, I think I still had all those joints in my sock the whole day! So, I came into the band with a pocket full of acid and a sock full of joints. But by then, these guys were doing Maharishi "OM" stuff and I think I ruined a couple weeks of their lives by being the "drug guy" in the band. As I remember they partook a couple of times with me but for them it was a throwback. It wasn't long before it was also the end of that particular period for me as well.

After the audition Don and I jumped into his car, this big old bitchin' Mark IV Jaguar, and drove into Laurel Canyon to Frank Zappa's house. That's when I started getting nervous. Frank was a big deal to me. As far as music went, my two influences besides the blues, and some jazz were Beefheart and Zappa! So I'm going down to meet Frank Zappa and by now he was definitely more successful than Don. I think *Absolutely Free* had been done, I don't think *We're Only In It For The Money* had been released yet. So we go down to Frank's place - Tom Mix's old house in Laurel Canyon. There's tons of people hanging around in this big old log cabin and I'm pretty nervous. So we went downstairs and ran into Frank. He was very cordial and animated and there's people everywhere. Women were all over the place - what an experience!

It turns out Frank was trying to put together this Rock 'n' Roll Circus thing, which The Stones later put together without him. I don't know how many Rolling Stones were there at the time, but Mick Jagger certainly was, as were The Who and Marianne Faithful. She was so ripped she was drooling - but what a babe - I was star struck! It was funny because Jagger really didn't mean a whole lot to me at that point. I'd played all their tunes in various bands. To me he really wasn't a singer - he was a "star". But when I actually met him, all I can remember thinking is, "How could you be a star? You're too little!"

Downstairs at Frank's was the first time I saw Art Tripp. He had just joined the Mothers and he was playing drums. Frank was rehearsing some tunes with a string section, clarinets and various other session players. Also, there was a one lane bowling alley down there! Well being the acid-head I was - I'm almost hallucinating to suddenly be amongst Zappa and all these people! I ended up in this jam session in a circle of people about six or seven feet apart and we're playing "Be-Bop-a-Lu-La"! Don was to my immediate left wearing his big madhatter hat and to his immediate left was Mick Jagger and right around the circle all these people were playing, Frank included.

So I'm jamming with these guys almost too nervous to be able to move or breathe. I started to ease up after I noticed that Jagger seemed to be equally intimidated,. Then we went into Muddy Waters' "Rollin' & Tumblin'" and a couple of blues things and that was it. It was such a strange experience - somehow just out of nowhere I'm down in Hollywood meeting Frank Zappa and this whole entourage of famous people like Jagger, Marianne Faithful and Pete Townshend. What an audition! There I was 19 years old and I'm very taken with these big important people.

Subsequently, any time I was hanging out at Frank Zappa's Laurel Canyon house or later at his house on Woodrow Wilson, there was always at least 20 people roaming around without fail. Even if Frank wasn't involved - it was because of him and/or in spite of him. Whether he was just a generous guy letting people hang out, or he needed a circus around him to feel comfortable - I don't know. Frank was always downstairs in his studio. I was there often enough to get a feel for exactly how much work he actually did. The routine involved smoking Winstons, drinking coffee, eating peanut butter and jelly sandwiches and cutting tape.

As far as the general "freak scene" goes, I guess we were part of it, but we were pretty much locked within the intense environment of the band - 'hothouse kids' so to speak. As a result I didn't get out much to see what was happening on the streets. It seemed like everything, at least from my perspective, was centered around Frank. His label Straight had a number of artists on its roster including the Captain Beefheart band. Alice Cooper, as far as my first meetings with them was concerned, were some regular guys in jeans and T-shirts from Arizona somewhere. I never really got that feeling from them that they connected with Frank - it was just a record deal. The make-up and rest of it didn't seem to happen until a little later.

The GTO's I believe, were a Frank Zappa concoction and were pretty much tied to him. As was Wildman Fisher - Frank was basically all he had. Then, there was some other guy who used to sleep in an underpass and who had a name something like "Powerstation Jerry". He loved getting electric shocks and would go and hang out at the powerstation to get juiced! He also had the tendency to suspend himself in doorways - he was actually very strong. It was rumoured he was about

60 years old - but in reality it was hard to tell how old he was. He was obviously playing on a different field from the rest of us.

Right after I joined the band, I can remember going to this a club in LA a few times called Shelly's Mannehole owned by Shelly Manne the drummer. I was 19 and too young to be allowed in supposedly, but I got in anyway - lots of hair always helped! I remember seeing Keith Jarrett - this small afro'd man diving inside the grand piano pulling on strings and stuff. I'm pretty sure he was playing with Joe Henderson in a quintet. It was pretty exciting for me because a lot of the other things being played around then were pretty mainstream - and off he goes into a piano solo and starts diving into the piano - pretty cool!

Another group we had seen there was the Horace Silver band with Roy Brooks as drummer. He had a standard jazz set-up with an 8" by 12" tom-tom, and a 14" floor tom but with a metal mouthpiece with surgical tubing coming from it (this was 1968 remember) and going into each one of the two tom-toms. So, as he blew air into the tom tom, it would actually increase the pressure and elevate the pitch. It obviously had two holes in it - so he could blow either way into either drum. He was playing these melodic type fills and solos throughout the night. Being 19 and seeing this guy in his late 30's, blowing into his instrument and playing his butt off and coming up with this great stuff was the beginning of my acceptance of an artistic way of life.

That was really one of the best parts of being in the band. It legitimised art as opposed to that whole attitude of, "You're supposed to go to the post office and work and have three kids...." So when Don and I went to Shelly's Mannehole it always excited me because we were seeing the same people that we were listening to in the band. We saw Freddie Hubbard around the time he released his *Red Clay* album, and the tunes had a lot of eleventh chords. It had a very hard-edged African jazz/Coltrane influence, a sound that really got to me - for that matter it still does today. A lot of jazz in the post be-bop and cool periods in the late 60s had stronger, more angular rhythms. They weren't swinging all the time, maybe it was the rock influence.

I can't forget the time we went to Shelly's Mannehole and we got to talk to Muddy Waters. It was just Don and I who drove down there in his big Jag - he always had cool cars, and this was before he had the Hudson Commodor VI. This one time they had a blues evening at the club with Muddy Waters headlining. I was a big time blues fan and I hadn't seen Muddy before, so I'm excited about hangin' with Don and catching the real thing. At the end of the set he walks up to our table and he knows Don! I didn't know this, but they had jammed together before I joined the band. It became apparent to me that Muddy was actually intimidated by Don's presence. I remember Muddy saying, "Don I can't sing tonight I have a bad cold - I'm sorry." Well, maybe he did have the cold, but it was obvious that Muddy who was by then in his late 40's had gone out of his way to come over and explain the situation to this 28 year old pop artist. To see Muddy apologizing for his vocal ability to Don was a real eye opener for me. I grew up listening to Muddy Waters, Howlin' Wolf, Sonny Boy Williamson and to see how icons like these might be viewing Don gave credence to my hero worship of him. He had the voice and the power, I knew it and so did they!

CHAPTER THREE
Just Call Me Zoot

The early band rehearsals were mild compared to the intensity of later ones. But I wasn't to know that then. Perhaps the first indication of the direction the music was taking was when Jerry Handley left the band. I'll never forget him turning round and saying, "Where's the blues tunes?" By that time we were kinda beginning to push the edge - it wasn't *Trout Mask* material but it was on the outer edges of *Strictly Personal*.

I was starting to stretch out from a strictly blues mentality myself. Before I joined the band I had listened to a lot of John Coltrane, Miles Davis and Thelonius Monk. At that time within the band all those things were talked about as acceptable influences. Later on, all that was scrapped for the "art" of the band - seemingly condemning those jazz players for playing notes. Certainly, I was starting to embrace music which was a step farther out out on a limb, like Ornette Coleman, Albert Ayler, Stockhausen and Harry Partch.

Early on I learned some of the old songs - "Sugar & Spikes" and all the *Strictly Personal* material - I wasn't part of the *Mirror Man* album even though my photo ended up on the cover. The first thing Don wanted to do was re-record the entire *Strictly Personal* album. So for my first "official" recording session I was of course as nervous as hell. The studio had a cold feeling to it, kind of like a storage room in a typical grade school. Frank Zappa was the engineer/producer for the occasion, and this only added to my tension.

The amplifier of choice (not mine) was a Fender Dual Showman that was taller than me. We recorded three tunes; "Moonlight On Vermont", "Veteran's Day Poppy" and "Kandy Korn". The band was John French on drums, Jeff Cotton on guitar, Gary "magic" Marker, who had previously played with Ry Cooder in Taj Mahal's band on bass, and me on guitar.

"Moonlight On Vermont" and "Veteran's Day Poppy" ended up on *Trout Mask Replica*, I never heard "Kandy Korn" after that day. During the time we were rehearsing the rest of the tunes we got word from Victor, Don's cousin, that the album was already out! Sure enough, Victor showed up one day with it under his arm. Don exploded! He was in complete shock. The way I understood it from Don was that Bob Krasnow, the band's manager prior to me joining, had taken the master tapes and done a special number on them without anyone's permission. It being the time of LSD, accounted for all the phasing and so-called creative mixing. This was my first introduction to Mr Krasnow, and I have to say that in subsequent meetings it never got any better. John French might say differently - apparently on tour John would be in some shoe store and he'd say, "Man, those are great shoes", and Krasnow would go back and buy them for him and leave them in John's room.

My experience with Krasnow was altogether different. He just treated me like a little asshole and was extremely rude to me. But for a while he was big in the overall picture and pretty big buddies with Don, even after the business over the *Strictly Personal* tapes coming out, which indicated to me that Don couldn't have viewed it as that traumatic an experience.

I was pretty excited about the first set of tunes I was learning because they were a huge transition from the material on *Safe As Milk*, which at the ripe old age of 16 had blown me away to the extent that I knew all the tunes inside out - in fact, I still think it's a good album. The new material had that blues feel, but creatively had taken a large step forward. "On Tomorrow" was like an extension of "Abba Zaba", combining African and delta blues rhythms. The out-take recording of "Beatle Bones and Smokin' Stones", which I was learning my parts from, was just incredible. This was the first time I really got a sense of Don's powerful imagery, and the way he used the strings just killed me! With the amount of slide parts and the need for a very aggressive right hand technique, I was definitely geared up to play this stuff.

The early guitar parts carried the influence of former players, namely Alex St. Clair, Ry Cooder and Jerry McGee. There had also been another guitarist named Junior Medeo, a friend of Zappa's who only lasted a month or so. So it fell to Jeff Cotton to show me what to play and in some respects how to play it. Jeff definitely had his shit together, he knew both guitar parts to most of the tunes, and as always was very easy to work with. But if I may blow my own "Horn", I was a quick learner and slide playing, tunings, and finger style playing were not at all new to me. I did, however, have to get used to wearing those nasty metal finger picks that are generally used only for pedal steel. At first they were cumbersome and very painful to use, but after the bloody messy calluses healed, they became like "snap-on-tools". They were certainly very much part of the "Beefheart sound".

Contrary to what was written on *Trout Mask Replica*, I never played flute with the band. I brought it with me to the early rehearsals because I'd been playing it since highschool. I had practiced it to the point where I could play a few jazz standards like "Take 5". Basically, because I'd been played it in previous bands, I thought I knew how to play it.

Just as Zappa had given Don the name Captain Beefheart, so Don bestowed those of us in the Magic Band with our own nicknames. The name Zoot Horn Rollo came up quite early on. At first I thought, "What? I don't know if I like it". Then I had a change of heart and thought, "Oh whatever - I'm in the Beefheart band and this is the coolest thing on earth. I'm going to be rich and famous and I don't even have to go to college". I guess the name actually fit with this strange music we were playing and in time I felt pretty comfortable with it, and still do. I think it's actually quite cool. In that sense Don's way with words was lyrically beyond what I was able to hear - I was a music guy. So, the name was cool, but it wasn't like I was having to adopt a completely new identity because of it.

Jeff Cotton became "Antennae Jimmy Semens" on steel appendage guitar. Jeff and I went back a long way. Where I grew up there were three guitar players in town. The other two were a guy called Ron Peters and myself. Jeff had played in loads of bands. He was in Lancaster - I was in Palmdale. It was kinda like a Jessie James and Billy The Kid situation. It reminds me of the joke, "How many guitar players does it take to change a light bulb?" Answer: "One. And nine to say they could do it better". Then we started hanging around together and taking acid. I started turning him on to the bad things in life and that's when we became buddies. He was always a very high energy, intense guy and always very, very nice. I don't remember that much about us playing together - it was more about human aspects with Jeff.

So, there was that issue in the beginning - maybe it was just me. I'd hear the guy playing something and think, "God, I can't do that - what the hell is that?" and soon I would learn what "that" was.

Jeff definitely started to show more of the strain early on. He very quickly became intimidated by Don and lost his willpower (just like the rest of us did eventually). Certainly, by the time I joined the band Jeff was just so much more hyper compared to when I had known him previously. Through him I picked up some vibes that were very uncomfortable, only later did I understood why that was.

Then there was "The Mascara Snake" on bass clarinet and vocals. Victor Haydon was Don's cousin and was also a painter. He couldn't play a lick but had a lot of attitude. But merely wearing a plastic showercap and making clever comments didn't make him a player, at least as far as I was concerned. If I was to see Victor now I'd be tempted to say, "Hi - were you really in the band? What exactly did you do?!" We worked our asses off and he showed up with the "tude" and a horn. I'm not sure I would say that he played it, so much as pushed air through it.

Quite frankly it pissed me off. I appreciated his art and attitude in that sense - but there was something going on with him I didn't under-stand. Probably a very nice person but there was so much attitude you couldn't get to it. I was pissed off because he hadn't developed any talents on an instrument. Underneath it all, that remained important to me, no matter how much we were doing "art" as opposed to typical music.

I do remember early on we used to go up to this monastery where Victor lived in Chatsworth, CA. These monks would go around and do their "monk" thing, but then every Saturday night they would hold a talent show. We'd go up there and see some really creative stuff going on there. When I say creative, I mean like Wildman Fisher - really "out there". I don't think they were really trying to be funny, but we thought it was. They would have some very bizarre acts, including folk singers who'd do these eerie songs, and we'd just be cracking up thinking this is the funniest thing seeing these people who thought they were being deadly serious. There were a couple different people there who reminded me of Bette Davis in *Baby Jane* - way too much make-up, died blonde hair and probably 60 years old but acting like a voluptuous 34 year old. Very typical Hollywood.

It was there that we ran into this guy named Charles Manson and his troop of followers. He had this bus that he'd turned into a hippie wagon that people could live in. It definitely had that "Twin Peaks" feeling - that's the best way for me to describe it. This was just prior to all the bad stuff - the murders. It was in this dry stream bed just down the road from where Victor lived that they eventually found a body from one of his family's gory little numbers.

Mark Boston or "Rockette Morton" was on Bass and vocals. I'd been playing with Mark since I was 14 years old - he was as soft as a teddy bear. Some of my earliest musical memories were playing out at Mark's place. He had a garage that had been converted into a music room. His dad played pedal steel and worked in a grain factory. It was definitely very Country and Western at Mark's house. I'd come from a basically middle-class background - swimming pool in the backyard etc. Mark's situation was definitely not middle-class, he had a much tougher life going on. I spent a lot of time there, playing, partying, and hangin' out in the music room. I have a lot of fond memories of that time. At one point I learned a few country tunes that Mark's dad knew - it was so different playing something quietly and not with the typical "full volume" that I was used to.

Back in 1965 when we were in BC and the Cavemen it was hard to find people who played bass. It was considered the 'stupid instrument' - the guy who couldn't play guitar would play the bass. That was not the case with Mark - he was a good bass player. He also had the equipment and it made a big difference to the sound of the band.

John French or "Drumbo" was more distant than the rest, but nonetheless appeared to be on a more even-keel than someone like Jeff. I'd known John previously and always respected his drumming. There were two drummer Johns in town - John Parr and John French. John Parr was the jazzier of the two and later committed suicide at a very young age. John French has always been very consistent - very "right there". He probably wasn't part of the drug scene like I was when Jeff and I connected through all that.

By the time I had been in the Magic Band for six to eight months there was nothing tying us to the old days - it could truly be considered to be a whole new unit. But, it was really the beginning of the grind. The rehearsals were all about working on parts. Don was sometimes involved - checking things out - occasionally singing, but not that much. We all played through this amp that I brought with me to the house which was a six ten Silvertone - a beautiful piece of equipment. The whole band - bass, two guitars, and the vocal mike all went into this thing. I don't know what had happened to their amps and stuff. There were some "spare" guitars but basically the band, as far as equipment was concerned, was bankrupt.

As far as Don himself, in the early stages my relations with him were actually very good - it was exciting working with him. But it was increasingly clear that he was hard to get along with. He was a very creative force, but very soon I got a sense for the less positive feelings that were circulating in the band. As rehearsals went on, it got less and less exciting and more like drudgery - it was becoming extremely hard work. I was beginning to work my butt off!!! What I came to realize was that his creativity wasn't clear cut as far as being very musical. He adopted more of the mentality of a sculptor. His idea was to use sound, bodies and people as the tools. It was increasing clear that our job as his band was to turn it into sounds that were repeatable.

CHAPTER FOUR
Practicing Parts

A month or so ago I listened to *Trout Mask Replica* and I laughed my ass off. For the very first time in a very long time - at 48 years of age - it was actually funny to me. Of course that's not to say we didn't have some fun while we were doing it, but after that it was mostly connected with tragic memories and the extreme reactions of family and friends who would have that look in their eyes as if to say, "You did that?"

The first thing you have to remember about that particular period was that the *Trout Mask Replica* material was very different from what I had been expecting to play. By now, any thoughts that I had joined a basic blues band had been dispelled and I had to learn how to actually appreciate this new material we were playing.

I say material, because I am under no illusions that some people would find it hard to call *Trout Mask Replica* music. The best description I can come up with is to call it sound sculptures. It was both polyphonic and polyrhythmic - with some repeated shapes. We would play in various time signatures, often at the same time. For instance, one part might be in 3/4 time while another was in 4/4 time. Only when they touched down together after twelve beats, would we move on to the next section of the piece. Very rarely did we repeat whole sections - usually we'd move on after whatever length of time it took to get back to square one. This would often dictate the length of parts or sections. If it took five times to play through your section and the others took three (polyrhythmic figure 5:3) that's how it came out. You'd hold on to your part for dear life against the thrust of what everybody else was doing

The story that Don has always told about the *Trout Mask Replica* album is that it took him 8 hours at the piano to write the album, and 6 months to teach the band the music. Well, I'm afraid that's bullshit!!! Total bullshit. To say it took him 6 months to teach us the parts, when he couldn't even remember them ten minutes after he played them to us, is ridiculous. It's true that it probably only took him a certain amount of hours banging around on the piano to come up with the basic parts - and that's not to downplay the quality of those parts or what he was trying to get across. He was very much in control and had a vision - but at the time I was probably too lost in trying to figure out how the hell to play the things to know what that vision was.

The writing process started with Don banging out certain things on the piano. Other parts he would whistle - it is well known what a whistler Don was - he could blow smoke rings and whistle be-bop at the same time, it was his party trick. John French would then translate these parts into musical notation. I don't know exactly how he did it, but it actually ended up in formal notation.

We would all watch as this musical process evolved (Don loved an audience). I know John kept things as close as possible to what Don had pounded out on the piano. When I say pounding, I mean he was literally chiselling away, and I don't mean that necessarily in a derogatory way. It was just him trying to get a feel across. That's the best description I can come up with. Another way of looking at it might be to say that he didn't know what the fuck he was doing and he was beating the shit out of the piano and trying to turn it into something because he was an "artist". But, we'll settle for the former, ok!

At rehearsals John French would show us all these parts and then the first thing we had to do was to try and figure out how to play them. Some parts involved playing seven notes at a time - which is kind of difficult with only five fingers and six strings on a guitar! I would try to find a way to delete a note or invert things to make it into something as close as possible to the original. The results were these parts that had incredible width - sometimes I had to play with both hands on, or by putting my thumb on the face of the guitar so that all five fingers were on the fingerboard of the guitar.

I remember thinking - probably not a popular thought - that everything was built from a rhythmic sense. Certainly it was that rhythmic element which has remained the biggest musical influence I have assimilated from that time. My feeling was that the actual notes themselves were interchangeable - it really wouldn't have mattered a whole lot as long as they created the same effect.

As far as I could see, Don really didn't know anything about music in the conventional sense. He was not a composer or arranger, but a very intense conceptualist. So it took a great effort on everyone's behalf to create these "sculptures" from something that was written in a non-musical way. Of course, that's as far as the music was concerned - the lyrics were a whole other ball game.

Sometimes it was easy to grasp what Don wanted, especially when his influences were blues-based. But it all depended on the description we were given. Often he would get frustrated about his inability to communicate to us in a way that we could understand. Sometimes he would just use imagery, other times he would pick up an instrument himself. About the only thing I don't remember him playing very often was Mark's bass. But he could beat the shit out of a guitar - the result can best be described as Jackson Pollock trying to play John Lee Hooker. I showed him an A chord and he could do these little hammer things on the second fret - he could do that forever.

At times he wanted to hear something from us that we were too stiff or overwhelmed to play. But it was difficult just working from all these images. Sometimes I wished he could have said, "Well, it's an A

7th, and you do this and you do that". Using musical terms would have made things easier, but it would never have covered the whole concept and detracted from the bigger picture of what he was trying to get across. Also, to have told us directly what to play would have given us way too much control over the music. So he kept control by waiting until it sounded like something he liked, rather than something he intended. And I should underline that - he would work until it sounded right - not that he had any intention of it being a specific way, most of the time.

It could be a very frustrating process. I remember reading an interview with a later band member where the guy was talking about Don and describing "all these great artistic things" - to me it was a lot of hero worship bullshit. Yeh, he was creative and all that but he didn't come from another planet. When he tells you to "paint the room blue and imagine this", that's all very well - but using more than an image would have required a specific intention on his part, rather than the air of generality which left the players to shoulder the responsibility of interpretation!

So, most of the time the band acted as interpreters of Don's ideas. As far as contributing to the actual writing, occasionally I would pose the question, "Well I can't do this but what about this?" and the parts would get changed. But I can't really claim to have written any of the music. If I played something and Don said, "Yes, what was that?!", then it was included. The whole vibe consisted of us being enlightened by our overseer. There was just this constant overpowering feeling of, "We are playing music, practicing music - just music, music, music!!!" It was really hard for me to decipher boundaries. The whole process evolved in this hot house environment.

Behind the trees in the garden that can be seen on the back cover of the *Trout Mask Replica* album cover was this little laundry hut. One of my more vivid memories was being stuck out in this little shed practising "Veterans Day Poppy". I remember it was at least 100 degrees in there and Jeff and I were working on the guitar parts. For the first time the thought crossed my mind, "Oh no! Maybe this isn't going to be so cool after all".

I was becoming some kind of 'slavedog'. I remember sweating like a pig for about three hours working on parts that seemed impossible. In fact, they were impossible! In the end I would get about 80% of it, and then settle for the fact that it was about as good as I could do. And that's after practicing it for nine months! The worst part was that you never knew if a piece was finished, or how long it was going to be a tune and then changed. We were subject to Don's whims, let's say.

I don't think I quite understood the vibe within the band. Initially my thinking had been that we would practice a little bit, play some tunes, make a bunch of money and life would be this wonderful thing. I would be sitting back going, "This is fun, hey this is cool! We're gonna play gigs and stuff!" But it was soon evident that it wasn't like that at all - this was no normal group situation. The reality was, because we were playing virtually no gigs, we had no money. Life in the Magic Band seemed to consist of these gruelling marathon practice sessions - sometimes for up to 16 or 17 hours a day. Then I'd curl up in a corner on the floor and sleep, just to get up and practise some more.

But it was very difficult for me to complain about the situation. You have to remember that at the time Don was my hero, and when I joined the band he was doing the coolest music ever. I was living in such fear of going to Vietnam and dying. Instead I was not going to Vietnam, I was in a band, I was going to be famous, I was going to make money, I was going to get laid - all these wonderful things were going to happen. And as it turned out the main guy was just kicking my ass up and down the street.

As time went on, it was clear the *Trout Mask Replica* material was pushing all the parameters. Certainly, it changed my feelings about music in a real positive way. Those tunes became really magical to my ears - they felt like a part of me. It was all so new and I felt I was participating in something that defied description. I remember wondering how could I possibly describe this to someone, "What the hell do you call this?"

The equipment and guitars came from whatever I owned, and various guitars the band had sitting around at that time. Much of the time I ended up playing a Telecaster because I always liked the way it played. In comparison the Stratocaster's strings feel sloppy, especially when you have a strong right hand technique. We also had this instrument called a Mellobar - some kinda' weird ten string, half pedal steel, sling it around your neck slide thing. It was pretty strange, and because of that we felt it fit in with our profile. We kept trying to use this thing, but it never showed up on a recording.

CHAPTER FIVE
Smoking the "Beefheart" way

When we weren't rehearsing, Don would subject us to long sessions of being "brainwashed". In my opinion these sessions were a conscious decision on Don's part to create change. I don't think he deliberately sat down to brainwash us in the military sense of the word, but he was very aware of pushing us to the extreme. We might be in a room talking for up to twenty hours - that is no exaggeration, it happened - and at the end of that we were somehow supposed to have resolved something. He would end up telling us how he had gone through all of this just for us, and how exhausted he was - and I'm sure he was. I certainly was. But looking back on it, I can't really believe he was doing it for us, essentially he was doing it for himself.

There were several events in his childhood which had affected him deeply - particularly the early death of his father. Also, being an only child and very intelligent, I think he learned very early on about controlling people. It often appeared that he was carrying around a lot of hurt - not that we all don't - I just think Don's particular sensitivity carried it to another degree.

A lot of what he said at these sessions was motivated by his embarrassment of us. He would hone in on whatever it was that we were doing that he didn't approve of. Many of these were personal assaults on our weaknesses as human beings - from eating habits, to how we dressed, how we were sitting, our relationships with people. If he looked over and saw one of us not looking, acting or talking like he wanted us to, he was embarrassed by it. The best analogy I can make is when you are in a relationship with a woman and she's putting on some God-awful clothes to go out in. The problem is that you're going out with some people who you care about what they think. What do you do?

For instance, he was obsessively concerned with how to hold a cigarette. If you're hand was swinging from the wrist, it was apparently an example of how ignorant you were. Even though he used this same measuring stick on himself, we couldn't really care less about how to hold a cigarette. It was completely silly that we put up with that. I had to laugh when I was looking through some pictures for this book. I came across a picture of Mark and he was sitting there with his hand upturned because he had learned how to hold a cigarette "the Beefheart way".

Don's memory during these "brainwashing" sessions was remarkable. Often he would go off on a number of tangents, only suddenly to tie it back in with what he had been talking about originally. Quite often he would connect what he was saying to a funny incident that was actually happening at the time. For instance, someone could drop some baloney on the floor and all of a sudden he's got you out on the moon, talking about moon dust, and then eventually after an hour's conversation he could get you right back to square one and the baloney. He also had an amazing memory for people. He only had to meet them a couple of times and then ten years later he would be able to remember what they had talked about and strike up a conversation about the very same subject.

All this is not to imply that Don didn't also discuss his lyrical ideas and concepts with us. He would discuss them constantly. We were supposed to be his audience, which was great fun because it could be very creative and funny. I could see that in a positive sense, he would garner encouragement by getting the support of his little 'bandlings'. It was also like a brainstorming session. At the end of "Old Fart At Play" on *Trout Mask* you can hear Jeff Cotton say, "Oh man, that's so heavy" - meaning it was really deep of course.

But sometimes it would turn ugly and he would say things like, "you don't deserve the situation you're in". Sometimes you became the 'cool guy' that day, because you had played 4 notes that sounded good. If that was the case you would be used as a positive foil against whoever was the 'bad person' that day.

Recently I got together with John French, he was here visiting and my wife and I took him out to dinner, and he said a phrase I hadn't heard for years, it almost made me quiver. He said "You have a thing". And when you "had a thing" you were the culprit. The dirty thing you had done, whatever it was, was undermining the brilliance of our situation. So we all "had things", of course. Except one person - and you can guess who that was.

It would be about how well you played or the way you carried yourself as an artist. Anything and everything that was important to Don's artistic view of things. The guy was very brilliant and completely artistic, but he could also be a cruel manipulator that appeared to have no conscience in dealing with people. Of course for those of us who we were stupid enough to go along with it, we actually learned a tremendous amount along the way.

A lot of the talk was about artists like Andy Warhol, Jackson Pollock, Robert Rauschenberg and Willem De Kooning. He completely opened that world to me. More so than anybody else in my life. Don could talk at length about most artists from Monet to Modigliani and onwards. I remember Franz Klien being one of his favorites, (you can see a lot of that influence of black and white images in Don's paintings). These were all new names to me, the only ones I knew were baseball players like Sandy Koufax or Don Drysdale.

We would go to museums to look at paintings, often with Don's cousin Vic who was also a very good painter. It was as positive an experience as mind altering drugs were to me at that time. Don almost seemed to view life like it was an art cinema piece. He was a big fan of Ingmar Bergman - that black and white imagery again. In Bergman's films the sound was huge, when they walked across the leaves it sounded like a thunder storm. There was elements of that which connected to the songs we were playing at the time.

Another particular favorite subject of Don's was the psychology of an individual's relationship with their mother. Of course, as a person who had lost his father at such an early age, Don had let's say, a unique relationship with his mother Sue. In fact, his mother was always a sweetheart.

I can clearly remember going back to visit my mother up in Palmdale after one particularly gruelling session. We were driving around in this old pick-up truck and I looked across at her and said, "I can't like you right now", and she gave me the amazing response of, "Yeah, I understand." To this day my mother is one of my best buddies - and all this had come about from Don telling me that I was a "momma's boy" and that all the things that were wrong with me were were down to my parents.

The plus side of it was, that here I was - the typical middle-American, middle-of-the-road Billy - talking about my relationship with my mother and questioning things like that. Back in 1968 that was quite unusual. Nowadays, it might be pretty standard issue, but I don't think it was then. So I was thinking about things a lot deeper. All this combined with the sleep deprivation, food deprivation and listening to someone talk for hours, I got to look at things in a way that I would never have looked at otherwise. In hindsight I really learned a lot.

To be honest, most of the time around *Trout Mask*, we relied on hand-outs for money. Don's mother Sue, and his grandmother "Granny", definitely sent us money all the time - who knows how much of it we saw? My mother also helped to pay the rent on the house in order to keep the band going - way too much money - something I didn't, and still don't feel good about! Don was a good sweet-talker and he got along fine with my mother whenever she would occasionally visit us - I don't think he ever met my dad, I'm not sure.

Obviously my mother was half-worried, but half-happy that at least I was doing something musical and involved in something I could care about other than smoking pot. But her financial support, which was a few grand she had stashed away for my college education fund, was now being used to pay our rent and so forth. I think outwardly she would have professed, "Oh, our son is doing well and he's recording and travelling." But inwardly she was probably thinking, "Why am I paying the rent, when they're supposed to be successful musicians?" My dad probably thought I was just plain nuts. I mean imagine it - he has a 19 year old kid and when the neighbors ask what this kid of his is doing, all he can do is hand them *Trout Mask Replica*! It was difficult enough playing the album to our own contemporaries - people that had degrees in music would throw up on the floor when they heard it - so heaven knows what the neighbors who went to church on Sunday thought.

CHAPTER SIX
The recording of Trout Mask Replica

Learning the material for *Trout Mask Replica* had been everything - a sometimes fun but often excruciating experience. Even so, after all that rehearsing, there were only two recording sessions for the whole album. Neither could exactly be described as standard studio set-ups. The first so-called "studio" was our living room at the house in Woodland Hills. We recorded on a stereo UHER deck with very few mics - maybe two mics on the drums and one on each of our instruments - and probably a small mixing board. Dick Kunc, Zappa's engineer who was overseeing proceedings, had this stuff in a suitcase, so it was my first experience with a porta-studio. Dick was a neighbor and had done some work on my guitars. He and Don became pretty good friends - "Captain Beerfart" he would affectionately call him from time to time.

For the second session we went into a regular studio in Glendale - I think it was the one that had the Phantom of the Opera pipe organ in it - and recorded 21 tracks in 4 hours! They mic'd everything up and we said "and" - then played the tune, "and" then the next one, "and" then the next one - and 4 hours later we were finished. And that is the truth, I don't remember any second takes other than when we false-started on a couple of occasions. It was just straight in, recorded, done. So there you have it.

If I had to express a preference between the two recording situations, I think I'd have to go for the studio because it felt more formal and it made it seem important. (After all, this was only my second experience in a studio). Also, it wasn't the same damn place I'd played in for 12 hours a day working on the same damn parts over and over and over again. If nothing else, the studio gave me an opportunity to get out of there for a while!

The story goes that Don felt he wasn't getting his money's worth by recording at home, so he got Zappa to move the band to a professional recording facility. Actually that sounds pretty right - or maybe Frank was trying just to record us on this little stereo piece of crap in order to get a natural feel - fun and games with Frank!

Once we were in the studio, it was again Dick Kunc's job to oversee the recording. I think Herb Cohen told him to keep the sessions short and to the point, "Ok, when you're going to these sessions we need you to be our man in there. Beefheart has a way of wasting studio time. So without upsetting him, we want you to kinda keep things moving so it doesn't get needlessly expensive". Dick had a Mr Wizard appearance like he was wearing a while lab coat. He looked very professional.

Another common story around that time is that Don asked Herb Cohen (Frank Zappa's manager) to hire a tree surgeon, because he thought the band's rehearsing was making the tree in the yard sick. That's not entirely true, because Don wouldn't have thought that it was the music that was making the tree in the yard sick. He would have considered that his music could do nothing but make the trees grow! But yes, he did do that, he did call about a sick tree. I was practising too much to pay that much attention to those kinds of things. I do remember the look on Frank and Herb's faces, the raised eyebrow, but nothing said. It was early on in the courting process, and sometimes at that stage people will do anything, while later on they'd probably have turned round and said, "You're crazy - to hell with the tree!"

Zappa's role in all this was as producer of the record. After all, it was to come out on his Straight label. But to be honest, I don't remember him doing much producing. I mean, how hard is it to sit there with Dick Kunc and record 21 first takes? As far as him having much to say, it was pretty casual. A word here or a word there, but not about how we were playing or what we were doing. I mean, he was hardly going to say, "Oh, on that fourth chord, you were slightly ahead of time" - yeh, right? He was probably giggling a lot, and trying to guess what we were going to do next.

The only specific input from Frank I can remember is the time during my first session with the band that I mentioned earlier, when he came out and ripped his hand across the knobs on my Showman amp and cranked it completely up. I thought I was gonna die from the volume as I stood there shredding out these slide parts. It was in G tuning capoed on the ninth fret, so it was way up the guitar and the effect was like shrapnel ripping my ears out! It was very *Spinal Tap*.

As far as my connection with Frank Zappa, he always seemed a very nice guy. Very cordial and very busy. I think we knew he was important to the band - I certainly did. I had a great deal of respect for him, no matter what was said behind the scenes. Both Frank Zappa and Captain Beefheart encompassed a lot of things that I didn't get from a John Coltrane or a Miles Davis. I think it was the departure from traditional music that I really liked.

I can remember one particular time when Frank helped out on more than a musical level. Living in Woodland Hills, with no money, eating our daily ration of soya beans - I came back from the store one day with some food I had lifted, and the reaction was, "Wow, that was cool!" So we made a decision, which Don was party to, that the four of us were gonna go to the Safeway store and steal some food. Well, as you can imagine - it being 1968 and John French with shaved eyebrows, both Mark and him with big afros, and Jeff and I with waist-length hair, painted nails etc - it stopped the store dead in its tracks. And that was before we were running around sticking bologna in our pants.

Well I got in there and I knew that there's two-way windows and that everyone was watching, so I freaked out! I said, "I'm not doing this!" I definitely remember turning to Jeff and saying, "This is crazy, this is not going to work". So anyway, they went through the line and bought some small item and of course, as we walk out the door, they're waiting for us with the cops. I mean good grief! And I had nothing on me because there was no way I was going to do it. But the other three did - John, Jeff and Mark - you know cheese and bologna, whatever would go down their shorts.

So we go to jail and our call was to Don - like Don had any money to bail us out of jail! So he called Frank. And it was no big deal to him to put up the thousand bucks or whatever it was to get us out of jail. But it was a typical 'Frank thing' where he did it and we never heard any more about it. Whether he was pissed off, or whether he thought it was humorous, or whether he thought he'd eventually get his money back - I don't know. All I know is Frank bailed us out and never bugged us about it! And of course Don would tell us later, "How could you be so stupid to go around stealing things?!" Conveniently he'd forgotten that originally he had told us that it was a good idea.

Another connection we made through Frank was with the infamous Cynthia Plaster-Caster. Cynthia's friend got you ready and Cynthia's job was to make a plaster cast of your penis. All I know, is that I saw her 2 or 3 times when she came up to the *Trout Mask* house. Maybe she thought, "Oh the Beefheart guys, they're weird - we can go over there and hang around them, maybe that would be cool!". So she arrived with her briefcase full of plaster casts of various people's penis's - Jimi Hendrix's looked more like a lump of white dog-doo, obviously he was not excited at the moment of being cast. Anyway there was no way I was volunteering for this. There was this vibe about the band - "Only lowly little rock guys do things like that. We're the Magic Band, we're art dudes - you know - we don't have penises!" Ok , just kidding about the last part.

Don and Frank were definitely the "old guys", they were both 29 and had known each other for some time, so they had a separate connection that we weren't privy to. From what I saw of their relationship, on the surface at least, it was just fine. Certainly I was impressed when they collaborated on "Willie The Pimp" (from *Hot Rats*). I remember thinking, "God it would be nice if we could do some blues-based things like that." By the time they collaborated again on *Bongo Fury* (1975) it's common knowledge that their relationship had become more strained.

After *Trout Mask Replica* came out, Don and Frank supposedly had a big 'falling out'. Don apparently accused Zappa of producing the album badly and trying to make him look like a freak. But surely Don knew what was happening the whole damn time - he heard the songs - he heard the recordings. So why was Don dissatisfied with the outcome of the album? He had heard the whole thing before it was released, so I don't really understand what he was complaining about!

I don't think Frank ever gave me a straight answer about what he thought of the album. I think he appreciated the collage effect of it - and the aspect that "there's no way this is ever happening anywhere else on any planet - anywhere". I think he realized all that and for that reason he liked what was going on, and I'm sure he respected moments of the musicianship too. But Frank's reaction is probably best typified by his usual response of, "Oh well, I have to go back to work". The implication was that serious people need to go back to work.

I suppose you could compare *Trout Mask Replica* to the work of Frank Zappa, but in comparison Zappa's music is very harmonic and easy to listen to. *Trout Mask Replica* is just not from a musical place. Unlike Frank, I know Don had some experience of psychedelic drugs. I remember I gave him some acid when I tried out for the band. But we weren't really psychedelic people. To tell you the truth the inside sleeve of *Trout Mask* was a little more psychedelic than I would have cared for - we were Maharishi art dudes - "OM". By the time we started the material for the album there were no drugs involved!

With Don it was more a case of whether or not he was naturally far-out? I'm sure he was naturally far-out, but he was also predictably far-out and he also tried to be far-out - all of those.

There's a famous picture of Einstein where he's wearing this fedora-type hat and a long coat and holding a cigarette. I remember soon after seeing the photo, Don started looking like that, exactly like that! I don't see any problem with coppin' a look, but this shows the way he could create an image - that very intelligent look. Don was capable of being as normal as the next person (as long as you were indoors), but mostly he knew how to "present" himself. None of this I saw as negative, it actually made life fun. I mean, what better way to appear like a genius than to dress like one! It came from a sense of being so goddamned concerned about his physical image - or about wanting to be perceived as a genius. But he had a sense of fashion no doubt about that.

Another side, however, was the only child who had lost his father very young. I think that dictated a lot of what came out of the man. That whole thing of John French's name not appearing on the *Trout Mask* cover. It was very typical Beefheart stuff. John worked his ass off on the album - you'll notice he's under the bridge there on the album cover - but just because he had just left the band, which he did on many occasions, he wasn't credited on the album sleeve.

Within the band, John was one of the few people that stuck up for himself and didn't get as wimped out as the rest of us. Many times his basic Christian beliefs brought him into conflict with other members of the band and caused friction. Behind his back, Don and I would say, "What's with that guy John? How can he be a Christian - what's the matter with him?" Being a non-Christian myself, it was really strange for me, because at that time I couldn't understand why everybody wasn't just like me. I'm sure he felt the same about me, how could I not be a Christian like he was. Later in life of course as I grew up I realized that there's lots of different views and beliefs and I learned to tolerate the things I didn't agree with. John and I have always remained good friends.

So it was to his credit that John didn't ditch or modify his beliefs just to fit in, but the result was that he left the band many times. John worked very hard - too hard sometimes. He also had a strange sense of humor, which was coupled with an almost dire seriousness. Every now and then his sense of humor would escape and then he would go back to his usual furrowed brow, with that questioning look of, "How does this work? What does this mean?"

CHAPTER SEVEN
Trout By Track

You'll pardon me, as I start to take you through the *Trout Mask Replica* album if I don't comment much on the lyrics. Everybody's got them to read if they want to, and my perspective on these songs is very much from what it was like to play them, learn them, and how they rated with the band - just the overall feeling of them. The words involved concepts that were definitely Don's thing. With a song like "Old Fart At Play" I wasn't even there when Don went down to do the vocals.

"Frownland" was always a real fun tune to play. The opening lick was in 7/8 - although I probably wasn't aware of it at the time. But it had a real snap to it. But again like most of these tunes it had those broken sections to it, because everybody was playing in their own time signature, own key and coming together at some points and not at others.

The little blipping sounds on "The Dust Blows Forward N' Dust Blows Back" came from the cassette deck we were using out at the house being paused all the time. The incredibly floppy sound of the drums on most of the album can be explained by the cardboard cutouts John French had sitting on top of his drums and cymbals. These originated partly because we were always getting complaints from the neighbors about the noise, so the cardboard was a way of deadening the sound.

"Dachau Blues" was one of the tunes that rather then being humor-oriented or ecology-oriented - was definitely about World War II and Hitler. To tell you the truth I remember it the least. This was the only time we ever played it - other then the nine months rehearsing it! - we never played it live. Again I wasn't there when Don went down to do the vocals. In the end the voice completely covered up what the band had played. As I listen to it now, I can think, "Ok, why not?" But back then as a band member it was sort of like, "Gee, why did I even play on it when all you can hear is this bear of a voice covering up every single bit that we had worked so damn hard to learn?" So it was real frustrating, but then again it was pretty easy to be unified in what the message of the song was about, obviously.

"Ella Guru" was great because of the humorous aspect of it. We played it a few times live. The parts had a real chunky feel to them and there was a heavy laden rhythm feel that always felt comfortable to me. Even now, I like tempos where the pulse is slower.

As far as the little rap about rats and the stammer and all that - this was some guy that just showed up at the house, I can't remember why he was there, he wasn't a friend of anybody's. Maybe he was doing some work on the house or something. Anyway, he came into the kitchen and started telling this story and Don made him stop and repeat it so he could turn on the tape deck. This guy was up for it and just started telling us this story again. I guess he was probably in his late 40's - maybe as old as I am now - but we thought he was great. Quite frankly, it was great that we didn't have to be practising for another 20 minutes. It was a relief to have a few minutes off to listen to his story.

Typical of the recording at the house was "Hairpie Bake 1" ("Hair Pie Bake 2" was the same tune as Part 1 but recorded in the studio). Don and Victor were out in the weeds probably 50 yards from the house walking around playing their horns - which was where the sound of rustling leaves and the two kids that walked into the middle of the recording came from.

"Moonlight On Vermont" was one of the three tunes that we'd recorded on that first recording session with Frank Zappa before we'd really started working on any of the other *Trout Mask* material. It's obvious by the tone that I'm playing on notch eleven - the sound of those screeching Telecaster parts played way up the neck with a capo through this Showman amp that was as big as a hotel. After 30 years it's hard to untangle hindsight from what I actually felt at the time, but I can always remember loving this tune. As a guitar player there was a little more to hold on to - it was more of what I expected to be playing at the time.

Having said that, I was not real happy with how it came out on the album. There was an earlier recording of it done with Alex on guitar and Jeff playing my parts which had been recorded in the living room with the guitars real quiet and John just beating on some things. It just had this subtle feel to it and in comparison it just blew away what we did in the studio.

I had totally had forgotten about "Pachuco Cadaver" until I just listened to it again. It was another one that was fun to play because again we're all playing in a similar time and key - the guitar parts and drums are in sync - we actually played it as an instrumental later on. Then there's that bass part, which was something Don changed. I'm not sure what he was thinking, but it's completely in a different timing and sounds odd alongside us just playing regular stuff. So his part bugged me. As soon as we got to the next section it just moves really free and again we're in the same key. It was a real fun tune to play.

"Bill's Corpse" - guess who that's about? I think it was renamed for my morose mood at the time. Listen to the lyrics to it - it is real disjointed. Actually, it was probably one of Don's nicer gestures to reach out and say, "Hey, I'm naming a tune for you". I think he was trying to say, "You're acting like you're dead" - well, a lot of the time I felt like I was dead.

I don't remember "Sweet Sweet Bulbs" for anything in particular - except for working real hard on it. I remember it more for those nasty rehearsal times where it just felt like shit. So the tune never really brought any fond memories back to me.

"Neon Meate Dream Of A Octafish" was one of my favorite lyrical images. I don't believe it was ever played again after that - could have been. It was very hard to play the parts to that. But I liked how it all fit together. It was just as "outside" as any of them but that was one that really worked.

"China Pig" came about just totally off the cuff. Doug Moon was, if not the original guitar player for the Magic Band, one of the first three. He came down for a visit and was playing this straight ahead blues thing and Don really reacted to it in a positive way - almost turning around to us and saying, "Well, why don't you guys play this way?" We felt like saying, "Well we used to, but it's hard to remember how, since it's been 9 months of 12 hour days trying to do these other things". That had all gone by the wayside and I had totally forgotten how to play what I had been playing since the age of 13 - it just seemed out of context. I would never think to even play like that anymore. I had been totally changed by playing this other music - totally changed. I'm sure everybody else was too.

So anyway, Doug comes in and plays this simple A7 bluesy thing and Don starts doing these made-up things - just spouting off the lyrics. As I remember Jeff handed him one of his poems and he started running through something he'd previously written. Just as John was the music guy who doled out the parts, Jeff was the transcriber of lyrics. He was always sort of like Don's paper officer and that's why he wound up doing "The Blimp" and the voice on "Ella Guru". Again it was recorded on a little cassette deck in the living room at the house. Cassette decks were these new things at the time.

I'm pretty sure "My Human Gets Me Blues" is my all time favorite tune off *Trout Mask Replica*. It just ripped and it was fun to play. Actually it contained a lot of jazz elements - 'push beat syncopation'. At one point right after Jeff left, I was trying to invent ways to play these tunes and this was one of the ones that actually worked because I figured out a way to combine both guitar parts. It wasn't like polyrhythms or totally superimposed parts - they lined up ok. So I just wrote out where the two parts touched down and came up with a combination third part which was really fun to play. Like the rest of these tunes, it was a complete gymnastic routine. Two and a half minutes later and you felt like you'd climbed Mount Everest to get to the end of the tune!

"Dali's Car" was inspired by an exhibit we saw at an art exhibition at the LA County Museum. We got there and looked at all Salvador Dali's melted clocks and I thought that was really exceptional. But he had this old Model A or Model T car that he had filled with seashells and a mannequin - he had moss, slugs, and he had replaced the snails with paint inside their shells. He had all kinds of shit stuck in this car. It was just this damp smelly weird thing he'd done - it was very cool! The tune "Dali's Car" was a duet with Jeff and myself. It was this dissonant thing that was rhythmically very tight, and yeh, we could play it in our sleep all night long exactly like that everytime! In fact we would be so rehearsed and so in tune that it got too tight. We were so squeaky metallically tight that there was no life in it and it lost some of the freedom it had originally. That's why I re-did "Peon" (on Mallard's album) so as to put some air into it.

As I said before, "Hair Pie Bake 2" was a studio version of "Bake 1". On "Pena" there's Jeff Cotton again - the "paper guy" - reciting the poem and then doing his noise thing again. It hurt his voice so bad he'd be in tears at the end of making whatever that sound was. He had barely made it and was almost choking by the end.

"Pena" was one of those ones that fell into the category of tune that had repeats that were a lot more comfortable to play. It gave me something to hold on to. A lot of times you just played a part 4 times and you moved on to the next section. But don't get me wrong, these were really creative sounds and I wouldn't have wanted standard issue music, but a little variety would have been nice.

"Well", I don't need to talk about, because that was all Don.

"When Big Joan Sets Up" was like "My Human Gets Me Blues" in that rhythmically we were all playing to the same pulse. It also was one that we played live, so that was fun. Of course the more humorous tunes like "My Human Gets Me Blues", "Hair Pie", "Ella Guru", "When Big Joan Sets Up", "Sugar 'n' Spikes", "Moonlight On Vermont" were always a little more fun to relate to because we were able to play them live and the energy was easier to put across.

"Fallin' Ditch" also falls into the same category as "Pena", "Neon Meate Dream Of A Octafish", "Sweet Bulbs", "Bill's Corpse", "Dachau Blues" - tunes with parts to them that have no repeats and therefore hardly anything to hang on to. But usually there was something in each track that you could hold on to - connections that were really exciting! Especially to somebody's ears like mine that were more used to harmonic music. It made it all the more exciting because it created a sense of yearning, and when you got to the point where the parts all came together, it was even more satisfying. You know, it's like starving and all of a sudden somebody gives you a cheeseburger and you say, "Wow, this is cool!"

"Sugar N' Spikes", like "Moonlight On Vermont", was on that earlier demo tape I talked about made by the other band members before I joined. Subsequently, it was one of the first two tunes that I learned and maybe that's why I got connected to it. But the parts were really stretching out from the blues. It was like a blues band only with an orchestrated classical feel to it. One of the themes in the tune was lifted from a non-repeated line on *Sketches of Spain* by Miles Davis.

"Ant-Man-Bee" was easy to hang on to. It had a cool rhythm with basic blues parts. It was like "Hobo Chang Ba" and had that African feel. That was a new feel to me and was one of the great things I got from Don. I'd listened to Coltrane's "Africa Brass" but just never, ever got that feeling. John French put that African feel across because of the way he played drums. I can really understand why people when they listen to this say "What a drummer!" He was really ahead of his time.

Like on "The Dust Blows Forward N' The Dust Blows Back", "Orange Claw Hammer" has these clicking sounds between vocal passages. Don was just reciting the lyrics, and then throwing the pause button on to give him time to think about the next line. As I remember "Orange Claw Hammer" probably took two hours while the cassette was back paused and Don tried to figure out what else to say. He did have some stuff written down but a lot of it was done on the spot.

"Wild Life" was one of the coolest tunes of the batch to me and I just love the opening section. As I remember, it was the best horn playing Don did. Of course, he didn't know what he was doing but he got pretty good at squeezing out a great tone. Every once in a while when he found a note that he liked he would hang on it and on this particular tune it just fell into place pretty nicely. Not to say that he didn't play cool horn stuff. It's just when you're playing from an artistic mentality as opposed to a musical background, it can be iffy. The rhythmic pulse of that tune was really happening and the sentiment of course is easy to get behind.

I remember being uptight on "She's Too Much For My Mirror". Don sounds uptight when he's singing it. At the end, you can hear him saying, "Shit, I don't know how I'm gonna get that in there?", referring to the page of lyrics he still had left over to fit into the tune. This will show up heavily later, on *The Spotlight Kid* and bringing the tempos way down. This is something that could have been fixed if he had actually sung at rehearsals.

Gee, in hindsight, "Hobo Chang Ba" was pretty cool. Part of the tune was a riff from one of Don's other tunes and it ended up here. It had elements of the *Strictly Personal* tunes because the section was precise - in other words it featured some repeated sections.

"The Blimp" was Jeff Cotton reading a poem in Don's bedroom. Don was comfortably on his bed - not an unusual position for him to be in. Don wanted to call Frank and have Jeff recite this poem on the phone. So they called Frank - I believe they called him at home first and he wasn't there. Gail says, "He's in the studio", so they call the studio and he answers the phone. Frank was working on this tape with

Art Tripp and Roy Estrada playing this repetitive rhythmic pattern (which later became the basis of Zappa's piece "Charles Ives"). You can tell it's not us - just listen to the studio quality of the recording of those parts compared to the things we did. Maybe we didn't have that studio polish, but then again we weren't about studio polish, cardboard drums and tortured guitars was more us.

So Frank's working on this piece and Jeff calls him and says, "I'm going to read you this poem Don just wrote". So he just started reading it over the phone and Franks says, "Just a minute, let me turn on the recorder", and just started recording it. It just came together just by 'hap n' stance' - it just happened to be the tune Frank was working on when he took the call. After he finished, there was a very typical Frank response, "Ok that was nice - that's perfect - we can put it on the album just like that. Gotta go to work - Bye".

As I remember "Steal Softly Thru Snow" was one of the ones we actually did live that had some real difficult parts. I remember torturing myself to play the thing. But guess what - it's my favorite tune on the album. If I had to pick one tune from this album from my perspective - that's it! This is the tune that musically has the most to offer. The unison rhythm things and John French's playing on it is ripping! Harmonically it's cool - it's out there. The sentiments run from ecology, humor, art and just 'out there' free-form stuff. So there's this heavy, serious side to it as well. It's odd because there's a couple sections in there that are just a bit too major - major always has that yellow, happy thing going for it, so it's a little funny - while the whole tune has a strong, dark feel to it.

"Old Fart At Play" kills me everytime I listen to it - it's just funny as hell! Of all the poetry, this to me just demonstrates the best part of what Don had going for him. I mean his lyrics - the overstated, overmelodramatic delivery. It's timeless to me.

"Veteran's Day Poppy" was the first tune I worked on in the band and one of the ones that was recorded with repeat sections. Some of the parts in there are humorous, especially when he's talking about veterans and all the sentiment of losing people in the wars. Suffice to say that one of Don's favorite words was 'juxtaposition'. That section at the end was obviously tacked on later. Zappa showed me this major 7th chord - actually it comes out as a minor 9th - but I didn't know about relative major-minor stuff then. If you listen to the end section it's kind of Zappa-like.

CHAPTER EIGHT
It Must Be Good Because Somebody Recorded It

The *Trout Mask Replica* album was something I did when I was 19 years old. Now I'm a 48 years old, I wonder how many other people are asked all the time to comment that far back in their history? I've probably had every feeling there is about it, ranging from, "I'm a part of a monumental thing" to feelings of complete embarrassment. If I'm talking to somebody that understands it - a musician or some painter - it's easy, it's just something that happened. It was done and that's what was cool about it. Purely on a lyrical note, they are really cool poems, I've gotta' say that. Sometimes I question their jelling with what we were doing musically, but in some ways that's what Don wanted.

On the other side there is the reaction, "Hey Mom, what do you think of the latest record I did?" And in response they're ready to hospitalise you for being so crazy. It's a tough thing to deal with - it challenged and changed me tremendously. It certainly totally changed and legitimized how I felt about art in general. Now, the thing that's pretty tough to deal with, is the people who say, "Ah, you've recorded some music" and they go out and buy this album and the next time they see you they have that look on their face. I mean I mow my lawn just like everybody else and I go to work and I pay my bills. I teach guitar and I'm just this kind of normal guy. I love art and 'out-there' but I love being just as normal as hell also! So what do you do when your neighbor looks at you like that? Or when one of my guitar students realizes I was kinda famous and then goes and listens to this album.

At the time it was released I was too confused to know whether I was happy with it or not. I was too close to it, so I had incredibly mixed emotions about it. I had got to the point of thinking - "Ok, so we played it, and it must be good because somebody has recorded it". Underneath it all I probably still wanted us to be more of a blues band. But I'd been exposed to the power of the lyrical images and rehearsing music that was in three keys at one time, not to mention time signatures. When you keep going to the same place you find comfort there and I found comfort in those tunes. I knew every nook and crannie.

It's hard to have an opinion about the music when it was my lifestyle - that's almost all I knew at that point. I looked at everything from a musical perspective, whether it was thinking about a Jackson Pollock painting or listening to Ornette Coleman or Harry Partch. That's how it was - anything else - wasn't! So it wasn't really a case of thinking, "Oh the album was cool - we did a good job" or "It was mixed badly and we played well". It was my lifestyle.

Certainly the critics loved writing about it. Obviously it was an album for the critics and I think all of the criticism was valid. I mean the people that hated it - hated it. And the people that liked it - liked it. But I didn't care what they thought. I didn't give a shit. I thought we were the only hip people on the planet - 40 people and five were hamburgers - right. That's a real pessimistic asshole statement, but anyway....

As you can probably guess, we did not really tour this album - we even turned down the biggest festival of all time - Woodstock. Yes we were invited, but "No, let's not play there. It's just a bunch of drunken hippies sitting in the mud" was a certain person's reply.

In fact, in the beginning I can only really remember doing one gig! Being our first live gig, it scared the piss out of me. I can't remember if it was before *Trout Mask* or right after, but I think it was Jethro

Tull's first gig in LA. There were eight bands and we were second on the bill, the Mothers were headlining. I'll never forget Art Tripp with his green moustache and a pair of woman's underwear on his head with his ponytails poking out of the leg holes. The Mothers were almost aggressively hilarious. Most of the guys in that band seemed to be having fun and looked like they were in control, but in an outrageous sense. Of course, Frank was definitely the most controlled of all of them.

It was a big gig, but not a big crowd. I think there might have been a thousand people there. We were playing the *Trout Mask* tunes so it was out there. For those early gigs it was "red light", "red light", "red light" and then the word "and", then we'd play. The "and" fell on the beat of 4. It was there because there was not to be any counting between numbers - none of the usual "1,2,3,4". Amazingly those things were rehearsed so much that they were pretty consistent! We all played at the same nervous level and the tempos were pretty up there.

That's really the only gig that we played until we got invited to go to Europe in October 1969 to play the Amougies Festival in Belgium. By now, John French was out of the band so our roadie Jeff Burchell became the drummer. He was more of a 'hippie-in-the-park' bongo/conga player, and had no drum experience as such. So I proceeded to learn some of the drum parts and then show them to him. What a gutsy move of his to learn these drum parts when he hadn't played drums before.

Originally, the festival was supposed to be in France, but was moved over the border after problems getting government approval. There were tons of bands including the Art Ensemble of Chicago. All I can remember is playing in front of thousands of people huddled together in sleeping bags at three in the morning in this huge circus tent. It's 27 degrees out, and there's frost on my strings! It was Don, Victor, Mark, me and Jeff Burchell on drums. Frank was sitting in with us, because he was supposed to be the festival mc - a difficult job when he spoke no French and most of the audience spoke no English. Having Frank play with us made me a little more nervous than normal. I think we played five tunes - the five tunes Jeff knew and that was it. Pretty weird flying us all the way over there and playing one gig! Then we went over to England and Don did a bunch of shmoozing and interviews and stuff. I just went around looking for girls - hanging out and having a good time.

In London we went to a gig at The Speakeasy, at the time *the* place to be seen in London. Quite often any musicians that were in the club would get up and play. Personally, I didn't, but Mark actually sat in for a few numbers. Ginger Baker played, I remember his complexion was yellow, maybe it was his diet at the time. Both Jeff Beck and Jimmy Page were there too - and I'm assuming they weren't friends because they were on opposite sides of the room. I was a big fan of Jeff Beck, and we had seen him previously at The Shrine in LA. As a kid I had really liked his stuff with The Yardbirds, his playing was totally unique and vibrant.

Anyway, I remember meeting both of them, and it's funny because it reminded me of when I was growing up and the guitarists would always be acting like Jesse James - only instead of who was quickest on the draw it was who could play the most notes the fastest. It was all about who was the bad guy of guitar. Both of these guys were the "hot rods", Eric Clapton being the third British contender, but Page and Beck had a much darker feel to them.

Jimmy Page extended his hand to me like it was some kind of great honor to be meeting him, and Jeff Beck was playing the moody tough guy. It was real funny cos you could feel the vibe between them. It was a big thing for me meeting two of the so-called "Top 10" guitar players. But it was good going through that demystifying process because it got it out of my system early on. Later on it really didn't bother me anymore - I was no longer star struck.

In fact, I remember Led Zeppelin came to some of our shows. Particularly Robert Plant - he was a nutty, free-feeling guy with lots of money, lots of women, and party favors. He seemed to be a very nice guy and so opposite from the others. I also met Jimmy Page again - what a snob (at least then) - I mean, someone that plays a bunch of

standard issue guitar licks and he's 'God'. But Robert Plant was a casual guy - not some 'music guy' with pastey little hands and a big attitude. He was pretty cool and he showed up to a few gigs and really
lightened the atmosphere actually - he was a very pleasant guy. He was
probably over-the-top, but for us, anybody that was laughing that
much and having a good time was great!

On the whole, however, we were taught not to appreciate other
bands. Jazz musicians who were old or dead, they were considered to
be OK. But apart from The Mothers, the official line was that you appreciated no-one. I don't think that Don really appreciated anybody
that much out there. Personally, I found it real easy to appreciate
someone like Taj Mahal. I remember seeing him in a band with Ry
Cooder, Gary Marker (who played on one of our early sessions) and
Jesse Ed Davis on guitars. They were doing blues based stuff. God, it
was a great band. Little Feat I really liked although it was a little later
before they really took off. We had strong connections as Lowell
George was an ex-Mother, Roy Estrada was from the Mothers, Elliot
Ingber and Ritchie the drummer were both from The Fraternity of
Man.

Back in the States we were still turning down gigs, but that was
purely Don. The few fans we did have, were mainly those people who
had bought the albums. We did however have a lot of celebrity fans -
Mick Jagger would call up to find out what book of black magic Don
was reading at the time. Some of the Merry Pranksters were also big
fans. I remember these two guys were running from the law coming up
to the *Trout Mask* house and talking about the crazy anti-establishment
type things they were doing.

We also had regular visits from Ry Cooder and Jack Nitzsche who
would come over and we'd play some bluesy stuff. I didn't learn much
from Ry at that point but I did pick up some things later when we
toured with him. I had already been playing slide long before that but
he was really good at it. His right hand technique of muting really
came through.

CHAPTER NINE
A Favorite Album Of Mine

During my time in the band, *Lick My Decals Off Baby* was my favorite Magic Band album. In hindsight I may have a different opinion - but I liked it because it was an extension of the the creativity that *Trout Mask Replica* had, only the writing process had become more refined. As a result I felt a lot more connected to the music because I knew a whole lot more about it. Rather than it just being four people starting at the same time, ending at the same time, memorizing their parts, but just not connecting with each other, I felt like I knew who I was playing with,

As John French was no longer in the band, I had taken over his role as transcriber of the music. In other words I was given the rather daunting task of deciphering the parts that Don had put onto tape. As I started to take these tapes home to try to convert them into something playable, my role developed into that of arranger. Most of the time I would try to be as true to what was on the tape as possible, but I got the distinct feeling that I could have done anything to these parts and no-one would have noticed as long as it had a similar feel or rhythm to what was on the original tape.

In that I was now responsible for arranging the music, I had so much more control on *Decals* album. I knew every note and it gave me time to concentrate on the phrasing. I didn't feel like I had to wait and think about what somebody else was doing.

The other main difference from *Trout Mask Replica*, as far as I was concerned at least, was that Jeff Cotton had left the band. Jeff had always a slightly more hyper individual than the rest of us, and I think the pressure from Don quite simply affected him more. I would like to be able to say that he left for all the usual reasons like, "Oh I don't agree with the musical direction" or, "You guys smell bad" or whatever. But that was not the case. With Don there always was a "culprit", there always had to be a person for him to vent his "beef" of the moment onto. Don was always picking on whoever he deemed to be the "bad person" of that particular moment. This always rotated, all of us were in that position at one time or another, but Jeff had real trouble handling it.

As a result of this picking on people, it was not uncommon for us to literally go around beating the shit out of each other! On this one particular occasion Jeff got the shit beat out of him - I am glad to say that I wasn't to blame, although at various times Mark, John French and myself had laid into each other. The result was that Jeff ended up with two broken ribs! It was pretty devastating and it's very horrible to remember that experience.

Anyway, this was too much for him, so he left, and ended up living a few blocks away. I think we went around a couple of times to see him, but I haven't seen him in many, many years.

At first, Ian Underwood was going to play the second guitar - a strange choice considering he'd only played saxophone and keyboards with The Mothers. He knew a C chord in open position and that was about it. As far as I was concerned, it was tough enough having to learn all the second guitar parts from *Trout Mask*, without having to try and teach new ones to someone else! To his credit, Ian did really well learning the guitar parts. But it was hardly surprising that he got these migrane headaches and had to go downstairs and lay down for a while. He was a nice guy, but I don't know what the hell he was thinking.

So, for *Lick My Decals Off Baby* I ended up being the only guitar player on the record. This is probably another reason why I preferred it. Nothing against Jeff Cotton, I mean his playing was inspiring, and he was a good friend, but it was just easier to handle all of the shit being the only guitar player.

As I remember it, the record was recorded over a 2-week period at the Record Plant in LA with Phil Scheer as the engineer - who I think had worked previously with the Velvet Underground. I don't remember there being a whole lot of sessions, but definitely more than there had been for *Trout Mask* - there could hardly have been less!

Just before we started recording, it was decided that we needed John French's drumming, so Mark and I drove up to Lancaster, woke John up and told him he had to be in the band again. Somehow we convinced him to do it. So, we now had two drummers - Artie and John - which accounts for the propulsion! You can tell the dual drum parts - Artie on the right with his seamless playing and snare roll parts, John on the left with his tumbling explosive style. When they both played drums together it was always a powerful sound. In the end, John played all the main drum parts except for "Japan In A Dishpan", while Artie added extra percussive elements and also played all the marimba parts. Artie proved to be a real pillar of strength and his influence was considerable because of his musical background. He certainly helped me rhythmically and I got a big positive hit from him as an individual.

By this time Mark and I were living in different homes and we were thankfully not all crammed into the *Trout Mask* house. However, financially the situation hadn't improved and we were still not making any money! I'm sure Don's mother was still getting lots of phone calls to support us, as was my mother. My mother spent quite a few thousand!

CHAPTER TEN
Decals By Track

"Lick My Decals Off" is classic Don. We used every method of construction on this particular tune. The opening part was built from the drums, a line I was playing, and a drawn out blues line which came from one of Don's whistled parts. The middle section was customised from a *Trout Mask* guitar part. The outro was a piano part with a key change. The make or break of this one is the drums - Don spent considerable time with John on those parts - and I think it makes the tune.

"The Whole Kit 'n' Kaboodle and the Kitchen Sink" was supposed to be a unison line between Don and I, and if you listen to it you can tell it's not together. While we were rehearsing it, he kept saying that he wanted it to be "more intense and faster!" Well, of course it ended up being my fault when we got to record it and he couldn't keep up. "You played it too fast!", I was informed.

"Doctor Dark" is pure *Trout Mask* - the two sections of sus chords show the Coltrane influence and, as difficult as it was to play, I always liked it. I guess I had a good hold on it. The vocals I always loved, but then again Don touched down with the track and found the same key enough times to satisfy me anyway.

"I Love You, You Big Dummy" was constructed from a bunch of strung-out piano parts. The entire tune stayed in E flat, and both Mark and I tuned down to keep the low end happening. It stayed right there - it didn't move much.

"Peon" was worked out from me trying to figure out how to play Don's piano parts on the guitar. I was recording a lot of these things and then taking them home and transcribing them. I remember laying on the floor for hours - you'd get tired of a chair and then you move down a notch to a stool and then you'd be on the floor. You couldn't go any lower, so you stayed there. I did that for endless hours transcribing those parts. I remember trying to make sure that the bass parts were in the same key and see if it was noticed - it was, and Don did some changes to make it even more "in key". I remember wondering how much I could get away with - but I didn't purposely mess with any of the things he had done, it was already so much damn work. I just wanted to do it and be done with it.

"Peon" and "One Red Rose That I Mean" were taken from the same cassette of Don's piano parts. I knew when I was working them out that they were going to be different, and very melodic - although you never knew how things would end up. Don was real excited when he first heard what I came back with, and other than the couple of changes to Mark's part, he didn't change anything. In the end he decided to leave "Rose" as a solo piece. Both pieces were well received when played live.

"Smithsonian Institute Blues" was a throwback to earlier Beefheart stuff with the guitar tuned to drop D and the basic slide parts. The intro with the marimba parts and Mark's bass part couldn't have been better. The single note slide part was a conscious attempt on Don's part to force a swing line against the straight time. Again it was a learning experience for me and it was a look forward to "Big Eyed Beans From Venus". For the life of me, I can't remember how the "out parts" were constructed, it wasn't from the piano, so I think it must have been an on-the-spot chisel job.

"Flash Gordon's Ape" ended up totally different to how it started out, simply by virtue of the horn overdubs. I remember being a little upset, after all the major effort we put into playing all these parts and then you can't hear any of them because of the overdubs. Now, as I listen to it, I can hear that it was a good idea - I don't know whose idea it was, but it worked. It was another one of the difficult tunes with a whole lot of dense stuff going on. It was not rehearsed a lot, but I can certainly remember playing it live at Pepperland, but not anywhere else.

"Petrified Forest" was definitely *Trout Mask* all the way. Don's vocal touches down with the track in two definite places, the intro and in the middle. It reminds me of "Steal Softly Thru Snow" for that reason, and because Don particularly liked these two tunes. The opening chord with all the open strings again gives me the feeling of the jazz influence. This tune came basically from Don's piano parts and I loved the way it comes down on that little major chord at the end.

Not a lot of time was spent on "Space-Age Couple". I think that Don liked the lyrical ideas so much that he forced us into recording it quickly. The tune came from the same tape of piano parts as "I Love You Big Dummy". These two tunes being based in E flat minor, make it pretty easy to hear what Don was doing - if you play all the black keys on the piano it's easiest to hear the f sharp major and the E flat minor. I wouldn't go as far as to say that it was a throwaway tune but I am suspicious by it's position on the album. If you look at any album from those days, the strong cuts were usually placed first and last on sides 1 and 2. But usually buried away on the second or third to last tune on each side were the weaker tunes.

The texture to the percussion parts on "The Buggy Boogie Woogie", was achieved by sweeping Fender guitar cases with brooms. We mic'd up the guitar cases and then John and Artie just kept on sweepin'. I remember having to play about 30 takes on this tune. Usually in the recording studio it was a one or two take deal, but I just couldn't seem to play for shit that day. It was the first and only time I have ever gone through that! I don't think I've ever done more than four takes on anything since then. Don was sitting in the booth and wasn't satisfied with what I was doing and I just kept getting worse. Fortunately it didn't turn into one of the typical "you're a person from hell" type situations. Instead it just became humorous and we just stopped. I came back the next day and I think we kept the first take!

"Japan Is A Dishpan" became an instrumental after a couple of tries with lyrics. Much of the tune was pretty melodic, but it's real Beefheart and we often played it live. I always felt Don enjoyed the instrumentals as it gave him a break from doing the vocals. To be honest, he would quite often lose his place in a song. For instance, recently I heard a tape of the band in rehearsal and Don's stepping all over the solos, he's completely lost. There's him singing totally freeform, loudly going about his business, and the rest of the group are playing a note-by-note gymnastic arrangement. When it meshed it was fantastic, because it showed perfectly how the two different approaches could play together. But when it didn't work it was terrible.

"Bellerin' Plain" was also in E flat. The marimba and guitar unison part came from a whistled part that had been floating around for a while. Don always seemed to have a reservoir of his favorite lines - both musically and lyrically.

"I Wanna Find A Woman That'll Hold My Big Toe Till I Have To Go" was one of the more fun tunes on the album to play. The time signature that I'm playing is pretty much the driving force of the tune - the drums are in and out of it. Artie's marimba parts were in unison with me in places and real tight - it was always real easy to play parts with Artie. What happened on a lot on these songs is that I dictated the feel so that Artie could chase me. So whenever we played lines together, or at least rhythms together, it was always me pulling it along. Also there's another guitar part in there that we laid over to make it more melodic. Again, a real short tune, and I think we played it 2 or 3 times live. I remember whenever we played it, even in rehearsals, there was always an upbeat attitude about it.

The intro part to "The Clouds Are Full Of Wine (Not Whiskey Or Rhy)" was culled from all these piano lines that Don had played and I stuck them together in a linear fashion. They definitely retained his rhythmic feel but again he wasn't particularly aware of the order in which they should be stuck together.

When we went through it Artie would write his parts down note for note so he could play the lines. I mean why memorize it? Being a crazy guy, of course I did. One of the best parts of the *Lick My Decals Off, Baby* sessions was the unison line Artie Tripp (by then re-christened Ed Marimba) and I played on this tune. In fact, because of the way the marimba had to be mic'd up, we were playing in two different rooms, me playing through those God-awful big ass amps. As I listen to it now it's not quite as perfect and tight as I had imagined, but it's pretty interesting considering that Artie and I didn't even have visual contact. We were playing these real frenetic lines in complete unison - no time signature to count on - totally free-form.

The big thing about this tune for me was that it was the first time I got a good feel for complex, compound rhythms. If you listen to the vocals, drums and bass, of course it's all in 3/4. But my first guitar part after the unison line is in 4/4 and counter to it - it's hard to hear when everybody else is really emphasizing the 3/4. I was usually the steady pole and the other parts were moving around me, but in this instance it was the other way round. It was a new feel for me to actually hold it together in opposition to everybody else. On some of my parts, especially at the end, you can hear how my spindly little 20 year old fingers can't play all the notes - but if it had been too smooth it would have sounded like some old jazz fart.

CHAPTER ELEVEN
God's Golfball

In the end we spent a hell of a lot more money on *Decals* and I'm sure we went way over our budget, but nothing like what was being spent on a lot of albums around that time. Even so, the results still sounded puny and clouded. I have to take some of the responsibility for that. Having worked so hard learning to play the parts, I'd forgotten to concentrate on the overall sound - even now I consider it to be one of my weak points. Because I was always so concerned with which notes to play, I never thought, "How do I make the three notes I know sound good?" It was more a case of, "How do I learn more notes?" So although *Decals* was recorded in a reputable studio and was produced infinitely better than *Trout Mask*, in some people's eyes it suffered in comparison, merely because *Trout Mask* was the first one to have that powerful onslaught of material.

Amazingly, we made a TV commercial to promote the *Decals* album, although it was never aired. It was kind of typical for us to do something without thinking, "Is it really gonna work?". But it was Don's idea. We were in this little studio somewhere in Glendale and

Don had an idea of the images he wanted - Mark going across with the egg-beater and him kicking over the dough.

The main thrust of the commercial featured this announcer from channel 13 in LA. His name was Fred May and he did voice-overs for these shlocky commercials for small business's - 'Mel's Dinner Jackets' etc. He had just the coolest voice - it was just like Cal Worthington (LA car salesman who has starred in his own cheezy commercials over the past 20 years). So Don hired this guy to do the voiceover so it would have that same feel to it. Of course Fred May comes in with a raving toupee and some kind of a tuxedo with a weird tie. But he did a perfect job. He just went straight into it, "I need more reverb. Can you give me two clicks more bass at a 160 cycles." I mean he was Mr. Professional. It was hilarious - it was great! We were having a good time watching this guy. I can't believe Warner Bros paid for this, but they did!

The cover art was probably Don's idea. We'd rehearsed for this album in the big long huts on the Warner Bros' lot that had the sets of the old TV shows *High Chaparral* and *Bonanza*. It was kinda cool because one minute we'd be playing in the middle of a desert with a fake cactus and then we'd turn around and there would be a bar scene with sugar bottles, the kind that are used in the movies to break over people's heads. I think that gave Don the idea to use the hotel set for the album cover. It was interesting to see how they created the illusion of all this marble everywhere, but as soon as you walked through one of the doorways you'd see the back of the set with all the 2' by 4's lying around.

When the album came out, the press was mostly positive. As ever, there were those pop writers who liked The Archies or bands like that, and if they bothered to write about us at all, they would describe it as "this horrible stuff". But I think we kept the critics happy because we gave them something to write about. Our small but loyal fan base would no doubt have bought the record anyway, but in a lot of ways the main reason why it really didn't happen until later was because we still weren't playing live that much.

I have really no idea how that record, or any of the others for that matter, sold. Probably about 20,000 copies to date, for all I know. At the time I'm sure it sold next to nothing - so I can't imagine that the label was exactly happy with the record sales. But I don't really know, I never had any connection with anyone at the record label - that was very tightly controlled by Don.

If you look at the back of the *Decals* album cover it says "God's Golfball Productions" - well that was Don, our manager Grant Gibbs, an attorney Mark Greene, and an accountant Al Leifer. These guys basically created this situation where they owned us lock, stock, and barrel! There was a contract we signed which stated that we were now employees of the corporation - they owned everything. Don originally tried to create a situation where we couldn't even use the names! Only recently I found out through my attorney that I can actually still use the name Zoot Horn Rollo. Royalties were supposed to be doled out to us through the corporation, of which Don was the president. I remember getting charged by Al Leifer for doing my taxes, even though I never made any money. As part of the corporation he would show me that I had made this much money and by the way, "here's the bill for doing your taxes".

CHAPTER TWELVE
Controlled Environments

It was around the time of *Lick My Decals Off Baby* that Don married Janet Huck. I wasn't best man because it was done in a little courtroom in downtown LA. It was just Don, Jan, and me as the witness. As I remember they had to borrow a little ring from this old guy who was the Justice of the Peace. He had this little drawer he pulled out which had adjustable rings in there like the sort you get out of a gum machine.

Jan was nice. As time went on she took on Don's vibe. She very much responded towards his feelings - what he liked and disliked, his moodiness and so forth. But I never had any problems with Jan, she was always cordial. Don was very much connected to Jan, they were a couple, they were together constantly. She was his main friend.

I'll be honest, I probably had misgivings at the time about the fact that we had to pay money for her to go on the road with us, which seemed a little unfair, but there were many things that were unfair. Obviously I didn't go up to him and say, "Hey I'm not paying for your fucking wife to go on the road", but on the whole I can't remember more than two or three times that I had a problem with Jan. Unless I was creep of the week.

I actually went fishing with Don and Jan once. I grew up fishing, but Don was a real indoorsman - it was a very weird situation to see him out in a boat with a fishing pole. We were driving along in his '49 Hudson Commodor VI - another of his great cars. I should say I was driving - the three of us went many places and I always drove. Halfway between LA and Santa Cruz we stopped off at a little lake and rented a boat and started fishing. I actually caught a fish which freaked us all out! He had the look of, "What are you going to do with the fish on the end of the pole now?" For him it was more about just being in this laid back environment on the lake and having the scenery and everything. So picture this - Captain Beefheart on a lake fishing, no hint of a suntan - one of the better moments with him. It was a nice day.

Generally, Don was most happy in a controlled environment with special friends. When he went out to dinner, if it was a special restaurant with a special drink, that was great, but there needed to be something special about it. It was important to keep the group size small in order for the situation to be comfortable, contained and retain that air of specialness.

He didn't, however, respond too well to your average Hippy Joe coming up and saying, "Hey man you're cool". I didn't blame him for that. Usually we would end up sitting in a concealed booth, where he could be just as sweet and fun to be with as ever. I wouldn't go as far as saying he showed a great caring, I was too close to receive that. But if I was out of 5 bucks he probably would have given it to me. It was just a shame that there was the other side to him where he could be very abusive and very manipulative.

You could tell from his lyrics that Don obviously had a great sense of humour. It was amazing to see how he would build up friendships and interact with people outside of the band and in business generally. On the whole, outsiders accepted him pretty well. I think he had a lot of local friends and business acquaintances with whom he was more kindhearted than humorous.

One of the key people Don could relate to in a business capacity was Bill Shumow. From the first tour of the East Coast in '71 with Ry Cooder opening for us, Shumow was on the road with us from then on. He started off as a roadie for that first tour, but he took more and more control of the organisation of our tours thereafter. He became road manager with the responsibility of moving us from place to place and finally as manager he would book all the gigs. He also managed Ry Cooder a short time after this.

I think it was all credit to Shumow's business skill, that playing live became increasingly easy - he just did his job unassumingly. He was also a great car repair guy, so I was always bugging the hell out of him to fix my little Volvo.

Shumow's relationship with Don could be pretty extreme. During the period 1971 to 1973, it became Bill's job to provide whatever Don wanted. He was also the major player in the process of "WAKING DON UP". Whenever it was necessary on the road to get to the next gig, to the airport, the limo, the taxi or whatever, it was a monumental effort to get Don out of bed. He was quite simply the deepest, most voracious sleeper I have ever seen. I would literally jump up and down on his bed and he would not wake up - or at least he would appear not to wake up.

To be given this particular job was always an excruciating task, because you then became the asshole who was waking him up - even though we might be in danger of missing an entire gig because of him sleeping. Later when Jan came on tour with us it became less of an issue.

Elliott Ingber used to say how much it reminded him of being in the army. We'd get the call in the morning "We gotta go. We gotta go." We'd rush to get all our shit in the suitcases, grab our guitars and run down to the lobby - only to wait for an hour. Then we would start the process of rebooking flights while Don was still wherever he was. Sleeping.

Bill Shumow was very graceful about all this. His personality and strength never seemed to be diminished by all the shit he took from

Don. That's not to imply that all of Don's requests were crazy. Not at all! However, most ordinary people's reactions to some of the really extreme demands would have been to say "Fuck you". Shumow handled it all really gracefully. He took care of Don's requests unless he really felt he could talk him out of it.

Shumow never got caught up in that, "You're an asshole 'cos you can't hold a cigarette right" scenario. For that reason I had immense respect for him. He also brought his wife, Michelle, and his son Chris on tour and they were a sort of side show to the main entourage. Chris was maybe 3-5 years old and we renamed him "Baby Shumow" - later they added "Baby Brazil". I really liked this because it added some normalcy to the situation - having a wife and kids around. They did normal things like going out for meals and having normal conversations. Not all this intense art shit that the rest of us talked about.

Shumow's life on the road was totally different to mine. My main task was to be "music monitor". I had to have a cassette deck ready at all times - Don would ring me at three in the morning and be whistling a part or a song idea, and I had to jump to it. Sometimes it was simply a case of being told, "bring your guitar down to my room." So that's how normal my life was.

On the road Mark and I were probably closest, because we were to be relied upon to carry out "Don's wishes". Roy, Art, Elliot and Alex kept themselves more to themselves. They weren't "on call" like I was. Alex could usually be found in the bar - not that all of us weren't at some stage - but I knew that I could find him there.

Alex St. Clair was unique figure to me because he had been the original guitarist with the Magic Band. With his one bad eye he had that real mean look - he looked as if he was going to pull a gun on you at any moment and I loved that. Over the years he lost that aura for me of the big, bad tough guy, and became one of those real sweethearted people. He probably still is, I haven't seen him in years and years.

My image of Alex was that he was one of the old guys and I would treat him like he was one of the original, classic blues players. The type that only know five licks, but God, are they good at it! They have this real power about them.

When we started working on parts together, his style stayed true to the early blues phrasings and it was really hard if I asked him to do things outside of that. Similarly with Elliot, I'd have to customise things to fit around his rhythmic eccentricities. My style was more inclined towards experimenting with technique and I had gone back to practicing a lot of pentatonic scales.

Over the years, we attracted a number of strange people who used to turn up on the road with us. We kept meeting these people who'd had these cool experiences. I remember a guy called Jean Pierre Hallett who hung around with us for a while. He had traveled, gone to Africa, lived with Pygmies and written books about it. He lost part of an arm on one of these trips. He he'd show us these photos, of himself in a pith helmet standing among all these people who were only 3-4 feet tall. Don was really into all this.

There was another guy, I don't remember his name, who was doing research into whales in the Bay of Huron. He had all these stories about living with the whales - kyaking around, hanging onto their dorsal fins, that sort of thing. These people definitely added to the mystique surrounding the band and to some extent the spirit of it as well. Don was really into the animal kingdom and ecology, which is evident from his lyrics.

There was also an artist called Neon Park who I met through Ted Alvy, a friend of mine at the time who later wrote some lyrics on the Mallard album. I really liked Marty's paintings - they were perfect squares, like album covers. One particular picture I liked had a Mexican feel and was based around this 'tomato in a hammock'. I guess a lot of these images came from mushroom induced trips. Unfortunately, there was no way I had $2,000 which was the asking price for the particular painting at the time. But I loved it and I wasn't surprised when it ended up as the artwork for Little Feat's *Waiting For Columbus* LP.

So, the coolest thing about being in the Beefheart band was that we didn't attract the same hangers-on as the Led Zeppelins of this world -

the hair bands with attitude and potatoes in their crotches. We had some thinking people around us that were into art, and were more closet-weirdo-nerdball types with a lot of quirkiness to them.

We also had a lot of connections outside of the normal rock crowd of musicians. Don was friendly with people like Ornette Coleman. I remember one particular occasion when Don was visiting Ornette and we were going to pick him up to take him to play this gig the band was playing at a Manhattan club. With us was the writer Langdon Winner and we were both in this taxicab with my three guitars in the back and Don's horns and stuff.

So, we pull up to Ornette's house on Prince Street, and I step out of the cab to go up to knock on the door. I'm standing there and all of a sudden I notice that Langdon's standing behind me because he really wants to go up to meet Ornette. And then we both turn around and notice the cab driver driving off with all of our instruments! And there goes my 1950's three digit Stratocaster - it was #360 or something, a Telecaster, Don's Mark IV Selmer Soprano and Tenor saxes. It was some bucks leaving in that cab! I don't blame Langdon for it, but I thought he was staying in the cab.

I ended up having to buy a guitar at a hawkshop, and borrowing another guitar from someone in the audience and of course with my very aggressive right hand technique I was ripping the strings off the bridge pieces - it was tough! It had to be the gig where Joe Henderson, Pharoah Sanders, Charles Mingus and Ornette Coleman had come to see us and I'm out of my mind because those were my idols!!!

CHAPTER THIRTEEN
An Emotional Low

By the time of the recording of *The Spotlight Kid*, Don had a really good notion of where to go. I think his basic idea was to return to his musical roots. Much of the inspiration came from the blues greats like Muddy Waters and some of those Howlin' Wolf tunes like "Natches Burnin'" or "Smokestack Lightnin". They are just so fragile and dripping tempo-wise that they are just barely hanging on. They have an incredible voodoo feel, they have magic! Things are falling apart, that's what really makes those tunes, and I think that's the feel that we were going for on this album.

Of course Warner Bros wanted us to make a more commercial album, but Don didn't respond to outside pressure at all. I think he had arrived at the conclusion himself that he actually wanted some money. Of course all of us wanted to have some money! We were all up for a change in direction, if it meant we'd get paid.

So, was the money any better? Well, at least we weren't borrowing from our mothers any longer - so it had to be a bit better. We continued to be taken care of by the God's Golfball Corporation and this meant we had a marginal amount of food money. Actually we all had to get food stamps, and wait in line at the government office for our allotment. We had all moved up to Santa Cruz and rented these little cabins in Ben Loman on Highway 9. There were six or seven of them stuck right on the San Lorenzo river there - each of us got our own little cubby hole.

I think the rehearsing for *The Spotlight Kid* was an emotional low for me. Sure, there were some great moments but they were few and far between. Without a doubt, this album nearly killed me. Even though the band was getting considerably good press at this time, I probably wasn't aware of it. This was Zoot Horn Rollo's "dark period". Like I told people for years this was my Vietnam!

It had got to the point where the band completely controlled every waking moment of my life. It was an amalgamation of things; leaving LA and being in a new environment, Don being very dissatisfied with the band, and the music changing because Don was not using piano so much to write parts. After 2 - 3 years of abuse and being "controlled", I was just a beaten little puppy and it really got to me. I had reached the cracking point where I had no self-esteem. Unlike Jeff Cotton, I didn't get the shit beat out of me, but I was thrown in a trash can - I think that was Don's intellectual way of telling me that I was garbage. It worked, I thought I was only worth trash.

I'm sure Don was very frustrated by everything too. Mostly, he didn't rehearse with the band - he'd just bitch and moan. By this time he had habitually become the 'brute' in order to get us to play what he wanted. And the more he kept bullying, the worse we got! He would have these temper tantrums and constantly yell and freak out at us. Suffice to say, there was always a culprit for Don to blame everything on and through his brainwashing he would get the rest of us on their case.

In the end *The Spotlight Kid* was recorded at the same studio with the same engineer as *Decals,* but it was done quicker. By the time we recorded it, I was in a little better frame of mind. As I listen to it now the tunes were conceptually well done, but I think the music was played and recorded anaemically. I thought there were some really good ideas and lyrics. I just wish I, or somebody else, had held their own in creating the music. It was another example of how Don could create a huge overview with great power and passion, but because he didn't know shit about music, he couldn't get things across.

I understand why Don wanted to slow the tempos down to create space for himself - or maybe it was a just an ego thing so he could be even more in control and be the 'front guy'. But I can't understand some of the album's mix, Don's harmonica is like the Empire State Building and the entire rest of the band are like a Volkswagen bus. The vocal ideas were getting very strong but they overpowered the band - we're just mixed out of everything. Maybe it's because he thought we sucked - perhaps we did! But the mix is just horrible.

I think the band had been beaten into submission and played like mummies. Remember the zombies in *Night Of The Living Dead* beating on the guy's house and chanting - well, that's a bit like what the band sounded like - we sounded dead. I recently spoke to someone who said it was his favorite album. The fact that it was so slow and dead was part of what he liked about it - unbelievable!

That's not to say that there weren't a lot of great ideas on that album, because it has elements of the older Beefheart stuff and retains the blues feel that needed to be there in my opinion, anytime. But it was so forced and uncomfortable it just didn't come off. To me, a lot of the things that people might think are 'Beefheart-isms' - those elements that separate it from other people's music - a lot of the time (not all the time) sound just like wimpish things that could have been improved upon. For instance, I can't pick out a particular thing about "There Ain't No Santa Claus On The Evenin' Stage" other than the sluggishness of it - the voodoo was almost there - but not quite.

CHAPTER FOURTEEN
In The Spotlight

John French wasn't in the band for all of *Spotlight Kid* but he played all the drum parts except for "Booglarize You" and "Glider". When we recorded "Glider", John French was the culprit that day and the "bad guy" - again this was all Don's crap. In my opinion John was playing just fine, but maybe Don had some idea in his head - who knows if it was musically possible or not - but it just became an issue. So we needed somebody to drum on this tune, and this poor guy Reese Clarke came in. He starts going, "Where's the basic A section and B section? Where's the groove? How do I play this?" Instead there's all of these strung-out repeated parts that went on forever. The song was so linear and this guy's having trouble following it. He was a nice guy, he came in and did the best he could.

The one interesting thing is how his parts sounded like conventional 'drums'. All of a sudden you can hear cymbals and tom-toms! It sounded strange compared to the way we recorded ourselves on previous albums, when we sounded like we were lost in cardboard! Again this goes back to us not concentrating on the sound. Our mentality came from the poetry - from sitting in a chair for 36 hours and listening to Don talk. Complete sleep deprivation and food deprivation - to the point where these sorts of feelings and questions don't relate. We became like those fuzzy little blue-grey dingleberries you get the bottom of your Levi's pockets - and it sounds like it on this album.

Odd as it is, "Click Clack" was done quickly. I think a lot of times the ones that you don't put a lot of time and care into come out clean and inspired. The ones you work to death, which for the most part the tunes on this album were, don't come out so good. "Glider" was certainly one of those 'worked-to-death' tunes - all those riffs. In the rehearsing stages it had a bigger, fatter sound which we were all excited about, but we lost that by the time we got to recording it. At the end of the tune I'm doing dueling slides with myself. I find it kind of hard now to listen to my extraordinarily weak technique - but I guess I tried hard.

That's Elliot Ingber playing the E7 riff at the beginning of "I'm Gonna' Booglarize You Baby". In classic Captain Beefheart/Don style he picked up on what Elliot was doing at a rehearsal and started writing and whistling parts - imitating the sound of a slide guitar. He would whistle or use whatever descriptive terms he could come up with to work off of what Elliot was playing.

By having guys like Elliot Ingber in the band it started to break down that mono thinking of "Don's World". He was older and more established, having already played with Frank Zappa. Elliot was very much like Don in a way, he could play things that had a real unique feel to them. Actually I considered Elliot to be a blues encyclopaedia, he was a master of a ton of different styles. But because what we were doing was so rhythmically different, when he was recording his parts he could get lost.

I remember one time when we were out at the Record Plant in LA and Elliot's all fired up on Angel Dust. I feel OK talking about that now because I know he's now living the straight clean life down in Hollywood somewhere. But he would just be ripped and get lost, so it was my job to sit there in front of his amplifier with headphones on and cue him in for his parts - I was sort of the 'Guitar Doctor'. So I'm sitting there trying to deal with this man who's dancing around with these very wild expressions and really working hard, but at the same time he's really needing my assistance to hold him together while he's playing. I would count him in with my fingers - making big slashes on the downbeats. I would point on the guitar neck to where he should be playing, "No, down on the first fret" or, "Way up there on the 9th fret".

I was the designated music custodian, making sure everybody played things right. I was the 'starter' and 'stopper' and 'cue person' for the rest of the band because I knew the tunes better than anyone else. I even used to cue Don when to come in to sing, when to stop, etc. It actually led to me being called the 'band leader'. That was my job - although 'leader' is probably the wrong word, it was more like being the 'implementer'. From this point on I was the guy who'd rehearse the band - hire and fire people. At one point I counted that we'd gone through 27 members - an awful lot of guys in and out of this band!

"I'm Gonna' Booglarize You" got played an awful lot and was definitely part of our live show. Like "Click Clack" and "Alice In Blunderland" , "Booglarize You" was a staple part of the set on three basic tours - 1971, 1972 and 1973. I can specifically remember the band performing it on a German TV show called *Beat Club*. Like all TV shows at that time, they weren't ready for loudly performed music. Our type of music was designed to be played loud, it didn't have to be earsplitting, but it had to be played with a certain amount of volume just to push enough air to feel the excitement level of it - because we did have energy, no question about it!

I remember how difficult it was, beating the crap out of the instrument and jumping around, when you could hear people whispering over the low volume. Of course, today when you look at somebody doing a show like *The Tonight Show*, the drummer's behind a plexi-glass screen and there's amplitude going on. Back then live TV shows were only one step better than lip-synching. It always felt funny playing to 30-odd people who were clapping politely while the TV producer was trying to make it look like a crowd 500. It was a very sterile environment and of course the Magic Band came over as being totally 'over-the-top' with our look - I remember stumbling around on my high heeled green shoes.

The first part of "White Jam" is Art playing the piano and me doing the guitar part. We're trying to play in unison and it sounds kind of stiff. I showed him the guitar part and he'd write it out. "Wow!", I thought, "What a wild thing, he can read music!" It was originally taken from one of Don's piano parts - you can feel that from the rhythm - and that's about as nice as I can be about that! There's a nice little key change into this blues-based part at the end.

The striking thing to me now, is that Don's vocal kicks ass compared to any of the other stuff. On the two previous albums, if he could have found a tonal center to sing from, he probably would have shined better. When we were playing a simple little thing like "White Jam" - he obviously found it. This was an inkling of what the guy had. The vocals really shine. The falsetto part at the end - the tonality and the shape - he could sing!

Boy, listening to it now, what a laborious hunk of crap "Blabber n' Smoke" was. We started this tune from the guitar parts. In fact we never started from a vocal line, even if there was a vocal line it was set aside and the tune built from the guitars. In this case, the guitar riff came from a lick I was playing in the middle of rehearsals and we started turning it into a tune. But I sound dead as I'm playing it - the tune has no energy which is a shame because it probably could have had. What Don was trying to get across could have been fun, but we were just grinding to a halt. John on drums, Artie on marimba - it's just so slow and we're trying "sooooo hard".

Listening to "Blabber n' Smoke" now, I do get the feeling that Don had a good idea and that I was just too screwed-up to carry it through. To me, this tune and probably a couple others - "There Ain't No Santa Claus On The Evenin' Stage", "Glider", "Grow Fins" - were very stiffly and laboriously played. I think if we'd been given the freedom to say, "Fuck you, I'm going to play this and here it is", it would have had strength. Because lyrically and musically they had enough of a groove going for them.

"When It Blows Its Stacks" feels like we were walking through the tar-pits. The whole tune was supposed to be built on energy but it sounds dead. Don was so concerned about the tempos, he was no doubt thinking, "Those young boys go up there and play that stuff real fast". It was true, at that speed it would have been hard for him to cram all his poetry in there, so he was trying to hold us back. The result was that it just sludged us down into nowhere. Even Elliot's over-dubs, where he's flipping around in the minor pentatonic, couldn't add some juice to it. Only later, when we played it live at almost double the speed, did it sound great.

"Alice In Blunderland" featured a guitar solo by Elliot that I learned note for note when we played it live - I don't know why, I should have played my own. In fact, the original solo was very long, it was during one of those studio "high points". In the process of editing it down there were a couple of bad cuts, and you can hear where Elliot is playing low notes and then very high - not possible.

The guitar intro was taken from a piece written by Don on the piano. If you listen to it you can hear a real down-beat emphasis to it, even though they were up-beats. This was because of the way Don banged things out on the piano. His parts were rarely made up of single-notes. It was always two or three fingers pushing down! The section after that is definitely from one of Don's whistled parts. If you listen you'll notice the difference between the two.

"The Spotlight Kid" is a rip-off of an earlier tune. On this album there was a lot of that going on - trying to pick off and rework things that dated from earlier days. Again, the over-riding thing about this tune is the incredibly slow tempo. Being tired and laborious, it reflects how emotionally down I was. The problem was that the lick to "Spotlight Kid" was not meant to be played that slow, it was just ridiculous! These things just screeched to a grinding emotional halt.

"Click Clack" was the main tune we did live. It was such a pinnacle to the live show - it just worked! Obviously it was easy for us to get into. It's one of the only tunes on the album that has a tempo that works. "Booglarize You" had a good tempo - "White Jam" was a little slow - "Blabber n' Smoke", "When It Blows It's Stacks", and "The Spotlight Kid" are way too slow. Those three might even have been recorded the same day in the studio - I'm not sure. Having a boogie tune like "Click Clack" in 3/4 time was pretty cool. On the album it changes to 4/4 for the rest of the tune, but when we played it live we returned to the opening 3/4 part. God, just listening to it now I can just see the sweat pouring off my face and onto the fret board of those old clanky Telecasters I was playing then.

"Grow Fins" had great lyrics and was close to being a really good tune. I was getting into using that great effect - tremelo - at that time. There was another tune that was done at the same time called "Little Scratch" which didn't end up on *Spotlight Kid* but was included on the German reissue of the *Mirror Man* CD on Repertoire Records. If you compare them they're obviously pretty close. Listening to it now, the recording was just atrocious but the bluesy groove of the tune set up the vocals pretty well.

CHAPTER FIFTEEN
On The Road To The Albert Hall

One of the few gigs I can definitely remember from this time was at the Albert Hall in London. I almost couldn't relate to it because the place was packed. I don't know how many people the place holds - 3,000 or something like that - but I'm looking up at three balconies high and they're packed! We were used to opening up for bands like Jethro Tull, but on this occasion we were the headliners and for some reason that just didn't fit with what we were doing, having that many people in front of us.

At that point we used to open the show with "When It Blows Its Stacks" which was one of our stronger songs. It was this E 'pa-chunk-chunk' type tune, pretty simple actually. I was waiting to start the number from behind the curtains and I made the horrible mistake of not checking to see if my amp was on! The roadie, Danny, hadn't checked either. So anyway, I ran out from behind the curtains and just as they're announcing, "Here's Captain Beefheart and the Magic Band!" I go to hit this big fat E chord - and there's no sound! All of a sudden I become little Billy from Palmdale, California - feeling about 2ft 9' tall and thinking about my mommy because I've got this crowd of people in front of me and no sound! I've never been the typically bodacious extrovert, unlike many performing musicians. So when nothing happens, my life passes before me!

I don't know where it came from but I held my hand up, put my finger in the air as if to indicate, "Wait a minute I'm going to rectify this", and went back behind the curtain. I knew immediately what was wrong so I turned the amp on and ran out, paused just a second, and started the show again. I'm sure it seemed to the audience that it was done on purpose. I was totally freaked, but the crowd loved it!

Then Mark comes out wildly strumming his bass in unison with the riff that I had started. We were playing through these enormous amps, and being a real pro he wrapped his cord around his amp head, but the cord was slightly too short and didn't reach far enough to take him to the front of the stage. So, rather than unplugging his guitar - all it did was to pull his 7ft stack of amps down! Of course the roadies are jumping around trying to flip it up. So that was our entrance to our big gig!

After such a dramatic opening we settled down and ran through our normal set which included Slim Harpo's "King Bee", "Click Clack", "Abba Zaba", "Electricity". At this time there was definitely a lot of improvisation happening on stage, so we tended to play these tunes as they were slightly more stretchable or expandable. The other tunes, particularly those on *Trout* and *Decals*, were so exactly formed that they weren't easy to stretch out or improvise on.

On European tours we usually played universities - some really good gigs. Mostly I remember us being accepted much better in Europe than in the USA. We almost experienced what it must be like to have screaming fans - the point where appreciation of what your doing turns into totally silly adulation. It was really strange to feel that when it happened.

Other times life on the road had its problems. One time I remember arriving at a gig and promptly getting back on the bus and driving away. Don suddenly decided he didn't want to play the show for some reason. Maybe it was a horrible place, maybe he just didn't feel like playing - I don't know. Anyway, obviously it became a problem further down the line - about refunds and law suits and stuff - it wasn't the first or last time that happened.

The bus we were riding around in was pretty cool and I remember the driver telling me he was a mercenary in this very English accent. He was the nicest of guys and me being just a kid, I'm thinking, "What the hell is a mercenary? Is that some kind of religion or something?"

On the bus there was a bar in the back with seats that faced each other and tables in between. I remember playing a lot of gin rummy with Artie. I could usually hold my own but he was a tough gambler that guy. He was also an expert billiards player. One time I went out with Artie and he got into $100 dollar games with these gangster guys in Pittsburg with names like 'Frenchie'. The vibe was tense. Artie's going through the old routine of setting up his opponent by losing on purpose, he had the thing down to a tee! Needless to say he won in the end and came home with the money. It turned out that when he was a kid in Pittsburg he used to rack the pool balls for those fat type cigar smoking pool players for a dime.

I liked Artie because he pretty much held his own while the rest of us were being total wimps under the oppressive regime of Don's view of life. So it was neat to have someone around that was not so one dimensional. Also, Artie was a couple of years older and when you are 20 years old, a couple of years makes a big difference - now it's like he's the same age.

Art Tripp has a special place for me in that my respect for him and his musicianship has always been enormous. I guess it came from my mother always beating me in the head with "Gee, you never even went to college, you can't possibly know anything useful." Art would always take the time to show and explain things to me. He was *really* different than me, being from Pittsburg on the East coast. He had a totally different hit on things. His whole mentality, artistic expression and collection of quirky insights fascinated me. He always tried to control his own environment. He had been involved with some pretty arty things before he joined the Beefheart band - he appreciated art, theatre, he had become a percussionist, he had played with John Cage - real outside stuff! I could have learned a lot from anyone in those days, but I chose to learn from Artie. He is still a real interesting guy and still a real good friend of mine.

Above: Three years old with cookie.
Below: Battle of the Bands, 1966. Me far right.

Above: With Captain Beefheart at the Bitter End in LA, in 1970.

Above: At the Winterland, San Francisco, 1973. Photo: Bill Cody.

Above: At the University of Pennsylvania, PA, 1972.

Opposite page
Top left: Don with Art Tripp.
Top right: Don with Jan at the Green Hall, New York City, February 1973.
Middle left: Art Tripp with Lowell George.
Middle right: Art Tripp (Ed Marimba) and Elliot Ingber (Winged Eel Fingerling), Long Beach, CA.
Bottom left: Art Tripp with Roy Estrada, University of Pennsylvania, PA, 1972.
Bottom right: Mark at the University of Pennsylvania, PA, holding a cigarette the Beefheart way.

(All photos courtesy of Jay Tripp).

Above and below: Don, Jan and Art Tripp at
The Spectrum, Philadelphia, October 1972.

Above: At Clearwell Castle, Wales with Mallard, 1975.

Above: Zoot now, 1998.

CHAPTER SIXTEEN
Circumstances

Around the time of *Clear Spot*, I would spend quite a lot of time hanging out with Don. I was single and it kind of suited Don to have me driving him here or there. Mark couldn't do it because he was married to Laurie, who had been Don's girlfriend up until the time he met Jan. Don and I would end up watching a lot of football together, particularly the year of the Miami Dolphins 17/0 season. When we were watching football, or just hanging out together, Don was less concerned with being so self-consciously clever. In fact he could be very soft and child-like when he wasn't living up to his image. I mean the guy was a totally different person when we were watching Larry Csonka trudge in for another three and half yards.

Obviously you can get from Don's lyrics that much of his humour was pictorially based, and he could be very funny in normal conversation or over a beer - when it was just me and him, or me him and Jan. Unfortunately, most of the rest of the time he was always on stage, by that I mean he was always aware of his image, and within that there was always the syndrome of there being a good person and a culprit.

Luckily, during the writing and rehearsing of *Clear Spot* I was more often than not the good person.

Don was partial to the odd beer, he was also the man who introduced me to Cognac. He had a taste for some of the finer things - expensive cigarettes and nice liqueurs. I remember many a time having a Drambuie or a Grand Marnier. His favorite was a French liqueur whose name escapes me - it would really coat the throat and ease the vocal chords. For my part, I became a sugar drink freak, after the intensity of playing on stage it was like, "Give me a Singapore Sling" cause I didn't like alcohol. I got into beer later.

I never saw Don lose it through alcohol or drugs. I think he kept that whole issue in a very good place For someone as volatile and extreme as he could be in other ways, it's amazing how he could be so well adjusted to the use of drugs. During my time with the band he actually showed no signs of abuse - from hangovers to getting wasted - none of the negative things that go with alcohol or drugs, that was never an issue. Right from the beginning we all smoked a fair amount of pot. John French told me that before I even joined the band, Don had taken a lot of acid - I mean a lot - I mean who didn't, it was no big deal. And I know on the road he ran into other mixtures of things that were, shall we say, a little darker, but while I was in the band we weren't major druggies

Clear Spot was recorded at the Warner Brothers' in-house studio. Rehearsals were usually painful. At best Don wasn't there half the time - either sleeping in his bedroom or off somewhere. When he was there we didn't get much rehearsing done because there was always a problem about something. Every once in a while it was great fun and when Don loosened up he would show what he never could on record - he would sing his ass off.

Right from the word go it was more professional. There was more money, it was a clean smelling studio and we could take time to record! So it was totally different, there was a big budget compared to the other LPs - more than two or three times as much. By now I was feeling stronger and I think the rest of the band felt that way too. Don's attitude towards us as a unit seemed to have improved. Not to say, of course there weren't numerous incidents, but it was still better than it was before. We still didn't have much money, but all of a sudden my clothes were cleaner and there was a few more of them. We were actually flying down to LA to record and staying in a hotel room which was nice and clean!

One of the factors that made a huge difference on *Clear Spot* was the presence of producer Ted Templeman. Ted came in and we performed the tunes for him. He was a very professional and personable guy. It was a vast difference after being in what Frank Zappa described as the 'anthropological' version of the band - in other words the *Trout Mask* album period. After that we had been through the low budget get-it-done-quick phase of *Decals,* and then the just-dead feeling of *The Spotlight Kid.* Ted was professional and actually did some arrangements which affected the way the tunes came together. Not in a huge way but he did make suggestions and changes.

Of course, Don had the final say on *Clear Spot*, as he had done on the previous albums. But to keep Ted Templeman on the project, I'm sure that he must have made some concessions. Of course, there were still all the usual band blow-ups and fights - the same old shit. This time however, I got the feeling that Ted had taken Don to one side and said something along the lines of, "I'm not going to put up with this."

We also started overdubbing parts for the first time - building tunes sonically in the studio. In some places there are actually tons of guitar parts, yet the actual parts themselves are so sparse, it doesn't feel like that. Because I never was that 'notey', the guitar parts were easy to build upon and work with.

Personally, I've never been one to think that overdubs are a bad thing. I have always thought you should use the studio like a studio. It's totally the opposite of playing live. A painter paints right over the top of something he doesn't like, why shouldn't a musician be able to do likewise? You know, Picasso had the paint brush, he does something shitty and he paints over it. I mean that's what happens. I've never been one to think, "Overdubs, oh that's not real" - bullshit. It's as real as playing live, it's just different. Just like these people who say computers aren't instruments - fuck you, of course they are. It might piss you off that somebody else can do something nice with a computer that took you 30 years to learn how to play - but the real question is, "Does it sound good or not?" It doesn't matter how you got there.

The final outcome was an album that, because of the production on it and the simpler tunes, really stands out. In my opinion it was not our best album, because you can't refute the fast painting approach of *Trout Mask* and *Decals*.

At first, *Clear Spot* was going to be called "Brown Star" and then we started working on the tune called "Clear Spot"and Don must have felt that it would be cool having that as the album's title. The idea for the see-through cover was Don's of course - great idea! The vinyl itself was also supposed to be clear but Warner Brothers decided that was way too expensive.

CHAPTER SEVENTEEN
Clear Spot

On "Low Yo Yo Stuff" - like most of the tunes on the *Clear Spot* album - there was no "piano music" involved at all. Nothing was written that way anymore. "Low Yo Yo Stuff" was a riff that I began playing and was carved out by Don. As I played the riff, Elliot played a very basic chord sequence behind it. It was so strange to hear that type of chord being played - it almost seemed like ancient history to the rest of us.

I should mention that some of these tunes were started and intended for *The Spotlight Kid*. "Low Yo Yo Stuff", "Circumstances", "Clear Spot" and "Sun Zoom Spark" were all from that batch of tunes. Fortunately they didn't make it and were completed later when we moved to Trinidad, California.

Although Elliot was around at the rehearsals of "Low Yo Yo Stuff", Mark played the other guitar parts on the actual recording. I think I'm playing 3 or 4 acoustic guitar parts - just fattening the tune up. It was all about making it sound big. To give Don his due, I think he was very aware of using music. He was always asking for a certain sound. He would say, "Play one of those chords". In hindsight it would be easy for me to let the abusive situations and the total lack of credit he gave any of the other band members color my opinions. After re-listening to this song, I would give Don a lot more credit for controlling the sound and using the resources that were there. But having said that, in chiselling off these tunes, it became a little more of a band effort. Although the tunes were written by Don, mostly through vocal imagery, more and more of the music was built from licks that were being played or being worked out by the band.

"Nowadays A Woman's Gotta Hit A Man" had a cool drum part by Artie. He could play anything. The guy was just so precise - not soulless but precise. It really affected the tunes and how this album sounded having Art on drums, marimbas and piano. Also, listening to this 25 years later, I'm impressed with Mark's guitar playing. Mark did amazingly well in switching from bass to guitar.

Hearing the horn parts on this track - they work, but I'm still not sure about them. As soon as I hear those horns and the Blackberries vocals I can't help thinking, "But we weren't a commercial band. These are not commercial tunes." They sound more commercial because they are recorded well, but they still have weird things about them. So part of me likes it, and part of me goes, "You know, it just didn't quite work with those horns."

Basically "Nowadays" is a one chord tune, underpinned by that Louisiana rhythm that Artie's playing. We could have built it up and made it real traditional sounding but I'm glad we didn't. When you listen to it, the strength and shape of the vocal comes through - Don comes in at all the right places. His voice uses that Teresa Brewer thing at the end - those 'hic-ups'. I think he said it was Teresa Brewer he got that from.

Of course, I shouldn't forget Roy Estrada's bass playing, it's traditional sounding bass and it's recorded well for those times. The bass and drums are so 'right-in-the-pocket' - centered. It makes it sound more commercial than it is - as opposed to the anxious shrapnel of the early days. It was nice having that strength at the bottom end instead of the "everybody over-the-top" attitude of earlier times. Maybe this tune lacked a bit of creativeness in places. I liked "Low Yo Yo Stuff" more, but that's me.

"Too Much Time" was obviously an attempt to be commercial, so I have all kinds of different feelings about it. It was supposed to have that Marvin Gaye and Al Green sound - whatever that is - but for me it didn't cut it. It needed just a few more lyrics than that. The one little hook in there where he starts talking, it's just not quite there, but it shows what the guy was really capable of vocally and it's amazing. It was just another inkling of what the guy could do any day of the week when the microphone wasn't on. I mean, I can't stress strongly enough that he really was a tremendous singer - a big ballsy voice, a sweet higher end, and he could get enough phlegm in his throat to get a double-stop type of sound - like a David Sanborn horn part.

Although Don had the ability to sing straight-ahead R&B, by the time we came back around to this sort of material, I think too many things had happened. Sometimes, you can be working on something for years, and then when you go back to trying something you did earlier, you don't have the spark or naiveté or whatever it takes to do it. If you'll pardon the pun, I think too much time had gone by for Don to sing just straight R&B.

As far as Russ Titleman playing guitar - the Bobby Womackish type guitar part on "Too Much Time" - it needed that. I was always forced to be as angular and hard-edged the whole time, so it was real hard for me to get loose and syrupy, which is more how I play now, or at least try to. So we got Russ Titleman to play the guitar part and it sounded right for the piece. But as a track it fell between two concepts. We should have played it exactly as straight R&B or accepted that we could not get close and kept the creativity.

We tried playing "Circumstances" live but it was a bitch for some reason - those leaps in it. I remember those stops - that's what was hard about it, keeping the time together when you're hyper-nervous on stage. But it was a pretty cool tune, although I imagine it must have been pretty hard for Artie to keep the drumming even.

Don really loved the phrase "My Head Is My Only House Unless It Rains" and rightfully so - it's pretty cool! I just remember him liking that so much. Phrases like that were a big deal to him. It was all about the power of the words. I know I've avoided talking about the lyrics much, because there's so many different interpretations to them, but Don did live and breathe those words and to me that was the best part of what the band was about. It's weird because normally I'm not a word guy at all, give me instrumental music anyday. But that phrase just overwhelmed me just listening to it, because I remember how much he loved it.

What a drum part on "Sun Zoom Spark"! I can't forget that - where he's doing the cowbell thing and the drum part all together. When we started working on this tune, I think a lot of it came from that drum part. Artie just sat down and was just fiddling around and suddenly Don went "Whoa!"

I haven't heard this album in a while and I'm actually listening to it and becoming a Beefheart fan again - pretty funny! The opening lick is Mark on 'car crash' guitar and it sounds great - it's perfect. I'm playing a Rickenbacker 12-string that we rented for this tune, it sounds like it's going through a chorus pedal, but I don't think they were invented then as far as guitar gear gizmos go - so I'm sure it's flanged.

I remember in the mix, when they took the bass out in the middle section, and I thought, "Don't take the bass away, it's got to have some bottom end!" Actually now, when I'm listening to it, it sounds pretty cool to clear it out like that. Don was particularly enamoured with "Sun Zoom Spark", and the lyric says it all. Wow! It was pretty positive! Tight little number, wasn't it?

"Clear Spot" was a cool tune. The cowbell part was by a percussionist in LA who was considered 'the guy'. He could fill a room with all his anvil cases of all these different African percussion instruments. So he was playing cowbell on this tune and to get rid of the clanky sound they wrapped gauze around the stick so you could just hear the tone. Then he'd hit it with the butt of the stick to get that 'clank clank' sound. It almost sounded like he was playing a Talking Drum by sliding his hand across the skin to get that tone.

It's a straight 4/4 tune, and tightly constructed like the rest of the tunes on this album. With Ted Templeman's help a lot of parts were 'nipped'. Obviously he wasn't going as far as to make us into some pop thing, but it cleaned up the edges. Anyway, the result was a cool, swampy thing. If we'd recorded it now, I'd probably play something other than those puny little slide parts. But that would be a mistake because I'd end up playing a whole bunch of notes. The beauty of a lot of the tunes was that they were never "over played".

The Joan Osbourne tune "Right Arm" is definitely taken from the song "Clear Spot". They gave Don credit for that although it was my basic guitar riff. You can't write a whole tune with one riff but it certainly influenced it.

Over the years "Crazy Little Thing" has been a favorite with my friends - you know the type of people you drink beer and throw darts with. They have always responded to it. When people who don't know anything about me - golf buddies or whoever - find out about my background, they start to buy the albums behind my back just to see what I used to do. This tune is one of the ones that comes up all the time. Some of the ones from *Spotlight Kid* also, but "Crazy Little Thing" has always proved to be a favorite.

The whole tune was played with a strumming of the right hand to get a powerful feeling. After six months with one of my guitar students, I get them to try and do this right hand technique. Hendrix sometimes played that way, with his thumb over the top. A good example of this technique is "Voodoo Chile" where Hendrix would play a single note lick but he'd have to strum it to get that muted sound. You can't just pick it, it sounds puny.

What I appreciate about the guitar parts, listening to "Crazy Little Thing", is the counterpoint provided by the interplay between the two guitars. One guitar's sliding up and one's sliding in the other direction and they're really weaving. It was kind of a real nice effect worked out by Don. If you listen to the first part it's definitely just me. Then there's the real E major corny melody - I'm not putting it down I'm just saying it's real 'major' sounding - which came from one of Don's whistled parts. You can hear it going from a guitarist-type of part to this melody part - and it works!

The rest of the parts were taken from Don saying, "Play a little slide thing here" or "higher" or "lower". Other than that, it was just me going, "Oh well, I'll do this." So the acoustic guitar part is me doing identical parts to just widen it up. And again we had the Blackberries singing backing vocals for us. I wasn't there for the session although it would have been fun. But, "No, no, no you can't go there", was what we were told.

"Long Neck Bottles" was supposed to be a boogie tune although it's fighting it a little bit. Boogie woogie is that odd rhythm between swing and straight, you can't shuffle the hi-hat, you have to keep it straight. Little Feat were really good at that. All the parts on this song were memorized except for Don's random harp playing. He played his butt off and it sounds great! It's too bad that the rest of the band weren't allowed that freedom. In retrospect I guess I should have claimed my territory and maybe I would have been allowed some freedom. But what with Ted and Don butting heads, it never happened.

I think the horns and the Blackberries helped, especially on this tune, because of the banter between the vocal and the background. But I have mixed feelings about the single note 'major-key' guitar lines because they are all over the place. They're memorized parts rather than being open ended lines or fills, which would have been more traditional. In a way, it might not have sounded so forced into place if we had been allowed more freedom - it might have had more life to it. Although I guess the advantage was that I didn't over-play things. You know, "Oh man it's guitar-penis time and I'll play everything I know" type of thing. Also, the memorized parts gave it a real cartoonish feel. They're almost like nursery rhymes. It's way out of place but that's what's kind of cool about it.

This album was the first time that I first remember playing the all important 'Power Chord'. This tune had it in there when I go up to the

IV chord and I'm just dangling there, while Roy is hanging on the I chord. It's the first time I remember playing that. As a guitar teacher it's kinda funny because people really think they can play well if they can move that one shape all over the neck. I even invented a tune called "Tuff Guy" that I teach these kids based on a pentatonic scale played all in power chords.

"Her Eyes Are A Blue Million Miles" has a pretty damn cool texture. I must be playing five or more parts on there - two mandolin tracks, three electric guitar tracks, and two or three acoustic tracks. Ted liked doubling things up and building up a track layer by layer. It's interesting that by doing this the individual guitar lines when played together create chord changes. I liked the texture of the guitars, they had that very quiet, muffled sound - like ducks on a pond. They're so quiet, almost like an electric guitar just barely electrified. The reason is that they mic'd the strings as I was playing. I remember Zappa did that a lot. I recall seeing him in the studio and he'd be playing these very fast pentatonic licks - the 'weedly weedlys' as he called them. By mic'ing the strings as well as the amplifier he'd get that real bright sound off his guitar.

I still think that another verse would have helped this tune out a little. It seems a verse or two short, doesn't it? The vocal hooks become repetitive, something I find a little bit in common with the whole album. "Her Eyes Are A Blue Million Miles" was the third of the three little love tunes. Listening to it now, this tune was infinitely better than "Too Much Time".

"Big Eyed Beans From Venus" was the tune that made me famous, right? That was absolutely great! This is the sort of material that I personally, and Mark and a lot of other people too, expected to be doing when we did *Trout Mask*. It has all the elements to me. When I initially joined the band, the first thing Jeff showed me was a delta blues rhythm. It was a right hand finger style thing that became the 'Beefheart rhythm'. And that's what this tune is based on.

Both Mark and I played the guitar parts which had these repeated sections but also had linear parts like a lot of the early material. Actually some of the guitar parts are very similar to "Electricity" from *Safe As Milk*. The vocals were a mixture of lyrics and poetry. At times completely serious and melodramatic mixed with total silliness! Then of course, there was that sentence, "Mr Zoot Horn Rollo play that long lunar note and let it float". Those immortal words - I'd like to thank him in large print for that moment in my life, because it's obviously put me in the position where I'm able to do this book. People are calling me and getting a hold of me via the internet. *Mojo* magazine determined that this was the fifth best guitar moment in rock history. I love that tune, I think it is just fucking great!

Don wrote the bass part to "Golden Birdies" and obviously it's Mark playing not Roy. I think Artie had written out the unison lines and might have been reading them. I had to memorize them when we played this live. It wasn't that big a deal, but I hadn't learned something that strange in a long time. Just to think of the amount of stuff I memorized back then, that's probably why I play so many free things now because it's completely the opposite. A few weeks before *Clear Spot* came out we did do a short 10 - 12 gig tour. Our show consisted of playing the entire album start to finish.

Listening to *Clear Spot* I guess I can understand why we had fans. It is much closer to pop music - it wasn't 'jazzers' playing stuff. Were we a rock band? Of course not, but as it ended up being recorded and stuck on vinyl, it was really well put together. As an album I certainly prefer it to *The Spotlight Kid* - it is well produced and has humorous elements to it. Some of it's a little sappy for me, even when I listen to it now.

Certainly, as far as I can remember, it sold a little more than previous albums. But a lot of that was probably due to the fact that we were touring much more. Of course, there was still no money - the band never made any money, ever! I think the album was well received by the critics, although some of them were starting to say we had 'sold out'. I've always questioned what that means. I mean if you weren't trying to sell the album, why record it?

Possibly older fans had problems with parts of it. I mean, for someone used to listening to "Dachau Blues", I doubt if they're going to make the transition to "Too Much Time" too easily. But I think we only lost a few of the fans from the radical beginnings - the type who would say, "Only play *Trout Mask!*" But we also got new fans. Gee, even my mom would listen to this album!

Just listening to the vocals, I can see why people thought Don was the greatest thing going. Even in the early days, when I used to see him and the Beefheart band were doing Howlin' Wolf and Muddy Waters' tunes, he created a very powerful image. Then of course there was his harp playing. Even then, as he was projecting this 'attitude', his harp playing really did stand out and propelled the band. In blues bands when the harp player can play rhythmically and have a big sound, man that's like a big keyboard and can really punctuate what's going on.

To totally diversify here for a second, the group Blues Traveller has this large man who plays harp. I imagine his chops are very good, but he plays so many notes it's incredibly boring. There's no space there, there's no shape - there's nothing. Don never did that. He played well within himself, played the high end à la Jimmy Reed - the top two holes and then the lower holes, the bends, the shapes and the double stops. He was a really good blues harp player and, especially listening to it now, he played the shit out of it. Not like the saxophone, where he was just pushing air and moving fingers without the knowledge of what the fingers were doing. Although, he even developed that to the point where he could recreate some really incredible harmonic overtones out of the thing - or whatever you call it when you overblow the horn and you get the high frequencies doubling up and stuff. But I think the blues harp was the one tell-tale thing saying, "Hey look, he was a blues guy and he really was good at it!" "Diddy Wah Diddy" (the first single by the band), and parts of *Safe As Milk* got real close to what the guy could do. "Circumstances" and some of the vocals on *Clear Spot* did too.

CHAPTER EIGHTEEN
Nowadays A Woman's Gotta Hit A Man

In a lot of ways the material on *Clear Spot* had been a direct response to the type of audience the Beefheart band attracted. The idea that Don had was that a lot of our audience were, and this I mean this in a positive sense, 'brainiac nerds'. And they were all guys - where were all the women? What we'd failed to realize was that women do not listen to *Trout Mask Replica* - at least very, very few.

We'd go to a show and all we'd see were these PhD students with horn-rimmed glasses and pens in their shirt pockets just frothing at the mouth at what we were doing! They were loving it and becoming fanatical. They weren't 'druggies' they were 'brainiacs'! We had a high quotient of nerds. There weren't babes coming to our shows, trust me. Certain people would show up at a lot of the gigs. We would play in Amsterdam and the same four people would show up in Atlanta a week later. There were even a group of people who'd show up at gigs with cardboard boxes on their heads dressed like computers.

As a result, most of this album lyrically - like "Nowadays A Woman's Gotta Hit A Man" and "Crazy Little Thing" - all have references to women in them. Don was as into women as most of us, maybe not like a Bill Clinton, but he decided that lyrically almost everything was going to be about women. It was a very conscious attempt to try and get through to the other half of a potential audience that we were leaving out. I remember having typical fights and screaming battles for hours about what we were doing wrong as far as women were concerned - 'we' meaning the band, not Don.

Yeh, of course we did get some groupies - and I don't want to go into the grotesque Holiday Inn sexcapades, but yeh definitely. One of my girlfriends at the time was a woman named Patrice Bellomo. She and her sister were in a band called the Bellomo Brothers, I think they became a porno rock band. Another time we were playing at this club and Ornette Coleman and Mingus had come to see us. There was this woman there who was wearing a girl scout uniform, which was kind of cool. She came backstage and introduced herself to me - I was a shy guy. So she grabs my guitar, the top with the turning keys and stuff, and sticks it in between her legs and crotch and starts humping my guitar. She then asked me if I wanted any cookies?

While I'm on the subject of sexcapades, I remember a particularly strange gig we played in a gymnasium in Boston. We showed up and the equipment was sitting up there but there was no sound check. To get to the stage we had to walk right through the middle of the audience accompanied by a few bodyguards to stop people grabbing at us - which was kind of lame but made us feel important. The stage was this 6 to 8 foot high big plywood construction at the end of the gymnasium. I'm sure it was an echo bin for everybody.

Anyway, it was very crowded and there were about 3,000 people jammed in on the floor right infront of us. So, we're playing along and Don gives me the nod as if to say, "Look what's going on down there!" As ever, I was onstage left and I came up to the front of the stage and looked off this 8 foot cliff at the people sitting on the floor and there's this couple humping away, and I thought, "Wow, that's shocking." But I couldn't look too long, for fear of losing concentration on playing the parts - if I noticed too much of anything I'd be totally lost. So back to business, and a little bit later I come up to the front of the stage again and this time there's three couples down there going at it! Well that's about all I could handle, I'm cracking up laughing and trying to play at the same time.

CHAPTER NINETEEN
Some Nights Were Better Than Others

By far the worst crowd I can remember was in Springfield, MA. We played in this small venue - about 1500 people. It was like a little basketball court. Well we played the gig and the audience decided that they were going to take over the building and party all night. They wanted us to stay and play with them. Well we needed to catch a plane to fly to the next gig. They didn't like that and started throwing full quarts of beer onto the stage. Then they started tearing up the drumset and stealing stuff! I wanted to be let out of the back gate but the security cop told me, "There's no way I'm letting you out the back!" In the end they made us walk through the crowd to get out of the place and into the little station wagon we had rented. We had to leave all of our equipment just sitting there, including our suitcases which were in one of the dressing rooms. At the next town we all had to go and buy some new clothes.

I thought playing colleges was the best because they were the right size - they weren't huge places like the ice skating rinks we used to play when we opened up for Jethro Tull. In those sorts of halls all you could hear was a partial mix of the other instruments, and a lot of my-self. For sound those gigs were the worst!

Of course, probably more than 60 or 70% of the audiences we played infront of, except for specific gigs, thought we were just plain mad. Early on, when we were an opening act and not big enough to draw our own audience, sometimes we'd be playing with whoever the headliner was, and we'd empty half the room immediately. We'd be playing these 2000 seater halls, and there would be 500 people left after two tunes.

I remember one particular gig at The Shrine in LA because some of my cousins and family were there. They were pretty much just straightforward nice people from a Mormon background and here they are going to see that troubled teenager Billy with all the drug problems of the sixties. I'm sure that it was proof to them, if they needed it, that I had gone nuts or taken too much LSD. At those shows there would be three or four people going nuts and screaming at us how great we were. It would be real interesting to meet with those guys now and see what they have done with their lives!

I don't know how I would have reacted to the intense situation of seeing a band performing *Trout Mask Replica*. I can totally understand why there are fanzines and newsgroups associated with us because to have been on the other side of the fence watching what we were doing must have been incredibly different and powerful. It must have run the full gamut of emotions from passionately great to the most weird, stupid crazy thing you could ever see - and we got all of those responses.

And of course we got booed. Don stopped quite a few a shows right in the middle, to point his finger at the audience, and start talking to them. He would deal directly with whoever was heckling - and he was pretty good at it as well! It was almost a bird-like response - Don would puff out his chest, his face would get wider, his neck would start bulging. He would point his finger and yell to the spotlighting crew, "Put the spotlight on him!" It may have been a little over the top, but what the hell? When you're on stage who needs that shit from other people? I have to admit I usually enjoyed his response to aggressive hecklers! It all added to his basic discomfort with being on the stage anyway.

Later on, as we started to play for our own audience, the heckling didn't occur so much as people knew what they were getting into. When you are doing something extreme, eventually you acquire people who can relate to what you're doing, because it separates them from the norm. It is the basis for the appreciation of anything beyond the merely pleasant, eventually the audience kinda attaches its own personality to it. So there were some vehemently positive people at our gigs especially on the 1972 and 1973 shows.

I don't entirely know what Don's perspective on performing live was, but I can't imagine that he was ever comfortable with it, to tell you the truth. I can only tell you what the effect on me was in that situation. I think there were great moments and people were mesmerised by him. At times he was able to create things on the fly that were tremendous, but conversely he could never do the same thing twice. Sometimes he didn't have to, if we were doing an impromptu version of "King Bee" it didn't take much, but if we were in the middle of a tune like "My Human Gets Me Blues" or "Ant Man Bee", I'd be standing there thinking, "C'mon do your part".

I have to say also that there was always something wrong. I can only recall two or three gigs where Don didn't complain about the monitor system - sometimes right in the middle of a tune. There was so much vibe going on in his body, you could see the intensity level. A lot of times it was painful to watch him, other times it was powerful, but it was always extreme. It just wasn't comfortable, it wasn't fluid, it was forced. Maybe it was just the whole deal of living up to being Captain Beefheart.

One of my favorite band stories happened when we were playing in New Orleans. Elliot Ingber was in the band at the time and we were coming out of the dressing room to go on stage and start the show. At that time the full band opened the show without Don and then he would come out during the opening tune. Well Elliot was in full cannabis attitude - unlike the rest of us - and as he was leaving the dress-

ing room, the door locked with the strap of his guitar caught in it. Elliot was so stoned he couldn't even figure out that to get himself loose
all he had to do was pull the strap off the guitar. He looked like a deer
caught in a car's headlights. He just stood there staring at me - almost
in tears wondering what he's going to do! So I suggested he take off
the strap and leave it in the door and let's go play. So for the first few
songs he held the guitar and played without a strap!

Elliot Ingber was undoubtedly the quirkiest guy in the whole band.
He had stayed totally true to his blues roots. He lived in this tiny apart-
ment on Melrose in Hollywood. It seemed like he'd lived there for so
long that his place was almost a stop on the Hollywood tourist bus
route, "There's Elliot's house"! For all I know he may even still live
there.

I loved hanging out with him because he would always show me
new ways of releasing me from some of the stiffness that surrounded
my playing. And he did it in such a soft way. He really respected me
and my playing, and I think felt a little sorry for me when I was so
down-trodden. I would go to his house and rehearse guitar parts, which
was always fun because it got me out of the really heavy atmosphere
of rehearsing in the studio or the band house.

One lasting image I have of Elliot is when I strolled into his hotel
room only to find him completely naked, crouched down on the bed in
almost a monkey-like pose, with that huge hair he had. And there he
was, eating sheets of baked seaweed, with it crumbling into his foot-
long beard. He looks me straight in the eye and says, "Zoot, man.
What's happenin'?"

He had a such cerebral sense of humor that sometimes he would say
something to me which would go right by me. And then about an hour
later I would get the joke. I was so taken with him. He even walked
like he was on his tiptoes all the time, it was almost like he didn't want
to hurt the surface of the ground. He was really a colourful person.

I will also never forget playing at Winterland 1973 for various reasons. We were just heading off for a European tour and I had ten or so
buddies come down from Eureka to San Francisco and I was running

around trying to get them tickets. I remember talking to Bill Graham and trying to get some free tickets from him. He wasn't budging - I guess he needed to make his ten bucks or what ever it was. Eventually I got them in though, so it was great to be playing a major gig with my friends in the audience. For once it was a relief to be thinking about something other than whether I was going to be the "bad guy" tonight, the one that ruined everything by playing badly.

That particular evening we were the opening act for John McLaughlin and the Mahavishnu Orchestra. I remember leaving the stage sweating like a pig, taking off the guitar, stripping off three layers of clothes - I always wore too many clothes. They started playing one of the tunes from *Birds Of Fire*, and I was standing in the dressing room being totally blown away. So I went to the stage, and there was Don and he was saying how they were doing this shit music. But I stood on the side of the stage with my mouth wide open. I particularly remember being blown away by the interplay between John McLaughlin and Billy Cobham - it was like they had this "other" energy. It wasn't just because he was playing a billion notes, which he was at the time, it was the sound. They were writing tunes that came from a place that I could relate to - it was powerful.

I also remember playing with Larry Coryell and Eleventh House as our opening act at the East Town Theatre in New York. He had Alphonse Mouzon on drums. Larry looked like he was around twelve years old although he was probably around forty at the time. He slung on one of those big Gibson Super 400's and he was just dwarfed by it. He was always kinda fun - I talked to him maybe four or five times and he'd say, "Hey you Beefheart guys what's goin on? Let's go out and play some music", and he'd go out there and rip out some stuff. And those guys were just damned good. Just because it wasn't atonal and polyrythmic with an attitude, didn't mean it wasn't good.

So there were times when we connected with other musicians, but a lot of the time we were kept in tow, so we weren't involved with as many of those things as we might have been. We weren't allowed much freedom and were kept away from anything that wasn't controlled by Don.

Even down to what we could and couldn't wear on stage. Certain things were no's - and to tell you the truth I never really had a problem with it. Even when it came down to somebody like me - weighing 138lbs and 6'5" - wearing gold lame shorts. People used to think I wore white stockings because my legs were so white and totally hairless. They looked like shaved PVC pipes. But basically Don dictated our look. A couple of times the band took a trip to Western Costumes in Hollywood. This was where all the movie people would go to get their stage clothes. I remember at one point I owned the ringmasters coat that Vincent Price wore in a movie.

At one time or another everybody in the band had one of those long black Quaker coats with 26 buttons. Don's outfit on *Trout Mask*, the big green thing with the fur collar and top hat came from there too. Up to joining the band, I had been a T-shirt and jeans kind of hippie kid, so all of that worked well for me.

When we got around to touring the *Clear Spot* material, John French had come back into the band and even Alex St. Clair rejoined right after this. This was by far the best live band, even when we played *Trout Mask*-ish type tunes of which we only did a few. The nature of Roy's bass playing caused us to play different tunes live. Roy was a very good bass player. He played 'bass' whereas Mark played it as if it were a guitar with low strings on it. Artie could also have handled anything. With this band we played two European tours and a lot of gigs in the States.

A typical set included "Alice In Blunderland", "Crazy Little Thing", "Clear Spot", "Sun Zoom Spark", "Low Yo Yo Stuff", "Nowadays A Woman's Gotta Hit A Man" (a few times), "Big Eyed Beans From Venus" (we played to death), "Abba Zaba", "Electricity", "Click Clack", "When It Blows Its Stacks", "Grow Fins" (a couple of times). We also got into adding some blues tunes. During this time Mark opened the shows with the bass line from "Hair Pie" and we came in with an instrumental version of "Pompadour Swamp". Henry Kaiser has informed me that "Pompadour Swamp" in later bands became "Suction Prints".

I think when played live the simpler songs came across better. "Click Clack" was one that came across strong in concert. Obviously any song which was received favorably by an audience, or one that didn't just scare the shit out of them and make them want to throw things at us, was more fun. Actually "My Human Gets Me Blues" as far as the more challenging stuff was pretty cool. I liked to play "Steal Softly Thru Snow". "Crazy Little Thing" was always fun because the parts were very guitaristic.

In fact, most of the time the shows were very exact - I think I maybe played three solos in a matter of two years. But the band sounded really good and was at its best when we had both drummers - John and Artie. They both stretched out a lot on their drum solos. They had these plastic toy hammers which had a high-pitched beep like squeezing a little bathtub toy. They'd go from the drums to beating everything on stage. So they're playing these things and then Art would still continue to play drums and John would be off tap dancing! John was working on his tap dancing skills at the time so it was pretty cool. It loosened up the show where we just didn't rip through 40 minutes of the tunes, leave the stage and piss people off because we hadn't played long enough.

CHAPTER TWENTY
Playing It Commercial

We changed labels for *Unconditionally Guaranteed* - the album eventually came out on Polygram instead of Warner Bros. It was at this time that the DiMartino brothers came into the picture, so I'm not sure if there was actually a record contract signed. That was always dealt with by Don - effectively we were signed to him.

We actually had a manager in the transition period between *Clear Spot* and *Unconditionally Guaranteed*, and he's the one who got us connected with the DiMartino brothers, who in the process got Don to sign a contract with them. The story goes that this manager of ours ended up being written out of the contract, totally dropped out of the deal. And he went in and got down on his knees begging these guys to let him in on the "big Beefheart deal", and they just cut him out. They just cold bloodedly took the thing away from him. And I remember Andy DiMartino coming up to me and distinctly telling me, "Oh we'll cover you on the parts you wrote, we'll make sure you get your publishing dues" and all that stuff. As the DiMartinos came in I'm not sure what happened to Don, he seemed to get weaker and weaker. All I remember was that in the process of writing that album the situation got worse and worse.

I don't necessarily blame Don, I don't think he was in control of the details, I don't think he cared. Obviously he wanted to control and own everything, and I'm sure he believed that he was justified in doing so, and in a very small way I agree with him. After all it was his creativity and vision, but in my opinion he should have shared the wealth!

Unconditionally Guaranteed was the culmination of a gradual change that had taken place over the previous albums, a move towards getting more and more commercial. I don't happen to think that this was necessarily due to pressure from the record company to get a hit. I think it was more likely Don's idea. If you look at the album cover and his little phrase "Love Over Gold" with the profile photo, I think he was liking the idea of making some money and being successful. It was his change - he wanted it.

The group was now me, Artie, Mark and Alex St. Clair. Because Alex had been an original member, Don couldn't be as oppressive with him as they were the same age and had been high school buddies. But the rest of us were getting older too and as a result putting up with less and less bullshit. By now it wasn't uncommon for me to tell Don to "fuck off!!!" I think it freaked him out that this was generally starting to happen and that he wasn't controlling the situation. Roy Estrada certainly wasn't able to put up with the shit anymore. "Why should I put up with all this grief for no money? Not worth it!" That's really all I remember about him leaving.

Roy had always been distant. Realizing how dramatic and weird it could be in the band, and coming from his own experiences as a professional musician with the Mothers, I think he kept his distance and protected his own space. He got *really* tired of all the crap, just like the rest of us. Don was a really powerful person, and Roy got pulled into it too. Consequently he would create his own environment almost separate to the band. It almost got to the point of us saying, "Where's Roy? Where the hell is he?"

Roy was a great laugher, he would always be giggling, although he had his strong, stern side. I spent a good deal of time with him, I think Roy and I became pretty good friends during the last tour we did together, hanging out and having a beer here and there. I respected his musicianship and his strengths as a bass player. Mark was a far more aggressive bass player, but Roy was really playing from that fundamental bass place.

God, he just played these real funky, fundamental things, and didn't actually play parts exactly how they were written. As we began to improvise more and more, I would be on the same side of the stage as Roy, so I got to hear him more. That created some musical things between us that I started responding to. Sometimes it took a supreme effort to pull me out of the image that I had created for myself in the band, and Roy was a very big part of that. It must have been a really tough experience for Roy in the Magic Band and I guess that's why he quit!

Personally, I didn't really care about the direction the music was taking so long as I didn't have to put up with anymore bullshit. I'm not sure that the tunes were necessarily non-Beefheartish, but they certainly weren't like *Trout Mask*. I think they had that 'Beefheart' element, but during the recording process it changed a lot. However, unlike other people, if you just listen to the tunes, I really don't see this album as being that big a radical change in musical direction. As the songs were put together, they ended up being real 'verse-chorus' orientated and I really don't like admitting this, but a lot of the guitar parts came from me.

Don was at rehearsals a lot more, which was a real change. We were at a beach house in Northern California owned by a restaurateur who rented the house out for private parties. It was a gorgeous location, rehearsing in this 40ft by 70ft room right on the beach. You could see the whales go by as they were migrating and so forth! So the band was kind of happy and we were thinking, "God, let's just do something and maybe we can pay the rent!" Some people might have said, "Oh man, they sold out!", but that was easy for them to say, they weren't still living off of mom's tit.

The rehearsals weren't wrought with the usual problems and there was less friction when Don was there. There was much less of, "This is fucked up" and "That is fucked up". And when it did happen it didn't last long. Even so, when Andy DiMartino was there he could sense the build up of years of bullshit and started trying to separate us. He actually thought he needed to do that, but it was unnecessary because Don was so separate from the band anyway.

Because Don was losing his power over the rest of the band, it weakened the project greatly. Not that I think his abusive ways were good in any way on a personal level, but on a musical level he was beginning to lose it. All along he had said that I was going to get some writer's royalties for my contribution to the end product. He kept saying, "I'll give you credit for writing these songs - I'll give you a percentage." Well of course none of that ever happened. No, I never wrote a whole tune, but a lot of the basic lines and ideas were mine!

CHAPTER TWENTY-ONE
Unconditionally Guaranteed

The recording sessions for *Unconditionally Guaranteed* were at Holly-wood Sound, LA and were actually pretty easy. Go in there - one or two takes - done - good enough. I wasn't there for the vocals and some of the overdubs. I didn't give a shit - I didn't want to be part of it. By the time we were actually recording the album it was "Fuck you, I'm out of here!!! I'm not going to put up with any shit. Maybe if you give me a big check I'll stay." But after realizing that I was never going to get any credit for the tunes, the break up was already in progress.

I remember playing "Upon The My-O-My" through a little Fender Champ amplifier with a microphone on it. Don would say, "Do that 'chuga-chuga' thing." After my slide solo, which I really like, he told me to play these little one note solo things. And then this ridiculous flute part comes in. At this point I'm really thinking, "Let me play the stuff instead of some old beard coming in playing imitation jazzbo flute crap!" All the horn and organ parts were typical of the sugary sweetening up of the track that was done at the recording sessions - wiping out any of the grit that might have been there in the first place. The vocals seem careful, in tune and in place - an unusual thing. All the Beefheart fans will just hate me for saying it, but if only he could have done that on the earlier records - and he could have.

"Sugar Bowl" is just an entire piece of shit. I remember thinking, "What the hell are we doing here? Is this The Archies? Horrible!" By that time I was almost feeling sorry for Don. I mean good God, what was he doing? I felt disconnected with the whole project and reached the point where I thought to myself, "Just do it". I can't remember if we were in the Musicians Union then or what, but all I was thinking was, "Make a few hundred bucks so I can put gas in the car and get out of here!" But what a piece of shit this song was - by far the worst thing I've ever played on.

I'm struck with a really weird feeling when remembering this album. No matter how abusive he was, I was beginning to feel sorry for Don. I got the feeling that something was going on with him that I was unaware of. However, it's difficult to keep feeling sorry for him after listening to "New Electric Ride" again, because it is terrible! I can just see Andy DiMartino dancing around the room, thinking he was involved in creating something wonderful. But he didn't know anything about us. If we'd have handed him *Trout Mask* he'd have probably committed suicide!

Was that Neil Diamond on "Magic Be"? It really sounds like a Neil Diamond song. It sounds like the sort of music that makes me want to puke, like Barry Manilow and that stuff. I mean give credit to the type of guy that can put out that crap and feel that way about life, but it's just the antithesis of anything I feel. It's like - whoooo! This song should have been sold to somebody else. But even on this, Don's ability to put phrases together was clever, but the song was just terrible. Maybe people think I'm being too hard - so let's put it this way, "Magic Be" is anything but magic.

"Happy Love Song" sounds encouraging - like a cross between Bruce Springsteen and the Rolling Stones. But it reminds me of the days I was in a cover band - the sort of bar band who play to people who have drunk too much beer and vomit on the floor. Been there. I never liked 'rock sax' it always has that weird 'crapo-rocko' tone.

I really like the cute little guitar intro I played on "Full Moon Hot Sun", a little delta blues lick with a crystal clear tone and my trebley little nervous top end. But Jesus Christ the song is bad! It is slightly reminiscent of *Safe As Milk* - but come to think of it, if we'd re-recorded *Safe As Milk* it would have just kicked this album's ass all over the street.

"I Got Love On My Mind" - now that's cool (he says sarcastically). It takes me back to the first time I took a hit of acid. It sounds like it's 1965 all over again and we've been listening to Arthur Lee's Love or the Strawberry Alarm Clock. It's so paisley, it's gross.

I remember Andy DiMartino jumping around the beach house to "This Is The Day" when we were rehearsing it. He was thinking that this was our "Stairway To Heaven". I mean, I didn't know what he was talking about - "what the fuck is a stairway to heaven?" It would be nice if I could somehow eliminate all that guitar crap I played in the middle, it's embarrassing. Some of it was general ideas from Don, but a lot of it is me just trying to improvise around what he wanted and it's really weak. The overwhelming feeling about these last two tunes was that we were ten years behind the times. I mean it's such early psychedelic Jefferson Airplane crap!

For about ten seconds there I was almost interested in the beginning of "Lazy Music". Probably because that was all my tune, musically anyway - embarrassingly so. Again I say listen to *Safe As Milk* and even some of the bootleg recordings done before that at the Family Dog in San Francisco in 1965 or 1966. If you listen to the material from that era, it is much more powerful and blues-edged. On this track Don's trying to be this softy or whatever. If he'd just put some bite on it a little more. It's just so retro for when it came out, it's pretty funny.

I get a different feeling from "Peaches". Maybe someone handed Don a copy of *Clear Spot* and he re-listened to "Long Neck Bottles" or "Crazy Little Thing". It doesn't have the background vocals but it has all the horns and crap on there. Like "Upon The My-O-My" and "Full Moon Hot Sun" it has the element of almost a Beefheartish type of tune.

The album when it was released was dedicated to Dwight Tindle, Don Schmitzerle, E.Y. Tuttle, Ed and Ann Starck, Auggie DiMartino and Merrymans of Moonstone Beach. Dwight Twindle was the guy in Arizona who got me ripped on acid at one of his private parties. Don Schmitzerle was president or vice president of WB records. E.Y. Tuttle was a chiropractor in Eureka, CA. And Sam Merrymen was the restaurant owner on Moonstone Beach who owned the house where we were rehearsing. Later he wanted a piece of the action, but I think all he got was that little mention at the bottom of the album.

Again if you look at the album cover it says, all songs composed by Don and Jan Van Vliet and Andy DiMartino. So Andy DiMartino got his name on the writer's royalties for the songs that I was supposedly getting some credit for. They created a three way deal, that's how the DiMartinos worked. Oh, and of course - the publishing was handled by his publishing company Honeysuckle. "Arranged by Andy DiMartino" - yeh right! The way I figured it, by Don putting his wife's name on it, he would end up getting two thirds of the the writing royalties and only have to give Andy DiMartino a third.

CHAPTER TWENTY-TWO
The End Of The Magic

Certainly it's weird to compare *Unconditionally Guaranteed* to earlier albums when I was so young and easily influenced. The overwhelming feeling I get now is of how badly things had deteriorated, it was just too bad. The music sucked, and I could sense a feeling of relief that I wasn't going to be doing this for much longer.

I think in a way we had already decided to break up while we were recording the album in LA. We had been through the growing experience of, "We're not putting up with this crap anymore!" So it was obvious it was just a sleazy situation, but we honored our commitments to finish the album.

I can remember sitting in one of the hotel rooms and we're all going, "Why are we doing this?" and just basically saying, "Fuck this, we can be the Magic Band - this is ridiculous - we're not getting paid, we're not making any money, the music sucks and we've got these Di-Martino jerks involved."

I really have no idea what Don's feelings towards us were. But we had had enough of him treating us like punching bags - I mean what a bunch of wimps we were!! It was almost like the abused wife who finally goes, "Oh well you've beaten me up 30 times, maybe I'll leave on number 31".

When we told Don we were leaving, his reaction was pretty much obvious, "You can't quit! We have a tour coming up!" Supposedly we had left him in the lurch five days before a major European tour. All I can say is that we weren't rehearsing for this tour. I'm sure he was just trying to cover himself and hide the shock he was feeling.

At the time I wanted the news to hurt him as badly as possible because of all the fucking pain he had caused me and everybody else. But there really wasn't a sense of, "We're quitting now to screw you up on some tour thing". After all, he had done the same thing to us plenty of times already - by then cancelling tours was standard issue. But his version was that he had to go play the tour and suffer because we had walked out on him. Well that's simply not the truth!! He could have cancelled - he could have done any number of things. He could have asked us to play it - but no, apparently we were all pricks!!!

Finally it was over, after six years of rip-offs, and the ridiculousness of seeing him in the big hotel and us in the little rooms and him saying, "I'm gonna give you some royalties." It's unfortunate, because over the years I wish I could have been a friend of his - there were moments of course, but in the end he made it impossible. The only real question is why the hell did we not split up years before that? I'll answer that by saying that Don Van Vliet was a truly great person. But he was also an abusive person - in equal parts.

CHAPTER TWENTY-THREE
Mallard

I was screwed in a major way throughout my time with the Magic Band, but I can't blame anyone else but myself for being so naive and not taking care of business. I received no money whatsoever from any of the Beefheart albums I played on. I realize now that to expect anything else out of the music business is silly. Back then most people I knew were so naive that we didn't know we were being screwed - nowadays you know you're being screwed and exactly how.

I think Don's attitude towards us as a band was that we had left him in the lurch. I mean he had his clever things to say in interviews, but I'm sure his feelings were hurt. Well, tough shit! He screwed us over so many times, I really couldn't have cared less. People took me to task for the things I said in different interviews, but I just didn't care. All I did was to respond to questions and answer them truthfully about what had happened. I remember doing a *Melody Maker* interview and they said I was disillusioned and so forth, maybe so. Perhaps I was a little over the top, but certainly I said nothing I'm embarrassed about, or feel that I misrepresented anything. To this day I don't think I've ever really represented the situation as bad as it really was. I've only just told certain parts of it.

When we split off from Don's corporation we went back up to Northern California where we had been living and decided to keep going as the Magic Band. But then we found out that we couldn't use the name. The point came where we had to do a press release or something so that's how Mallard came about. It came from the tune called "Mallard Ballad" which we'd been working on in rehearsal.

At first, Alex St Clair was part of Mallard, along with Art, Mark and me. John French was up there too, he was actually singing and Art was playing drums, and we were just trying to configure how it was going to work. A guy named Mark Marcellino, who was on the last Beefheart album, played keyboards.

Gradually everybody went, "Ugghhh, this isn't going to work", me included. So, through Bill Shumow, Mark reconnected with Ian Anderson from Jethro Tull and he dragged me down to the desert to record a song that Ian had written for the Magic Band. It truly was a nice gesture but the song wasn't happening. At the time, Ian was into riding motorbikes and I remember his management company called up to say that they were upset about him riding his spiffy motorbike on all these dirt tracks. Ian Anderson, their cash cow was riding a motorbike in the desert with these weird jerks from the Beefheart band! So anyway we just hung out playing darts in my room and drinking Lowenbraus and smoking cigarettes. Ian encouraged us to continue and it was then that I decided this was still a viable thing.

Ian was always a very nice man. He was a big person in the business (bigger than either Zappa or Beefheart) - when you sell out the LA Forum 3 days in a row you're a big artist! But he was very personable and he was very much in control - he worked his ass off. In that way he was similar to Frank Zappa. Probably a 20 hour a day guy and slept for about 4 hours. He would drink a beer or two and that was it - no drugs, very clean, very businesslike.

A band like Jethro Tull was never really an influence on us musically, because they were very grandiose, whereas we were much more blues based. But from my standpoint the guys in Jethro Tull were not only rich and famous, but also *very* good at what they did. When I saw the level of control and the work that went into their shows - what they presented to an audience - I was blown away. We worked hard on one tune at a time. They worked hard at stringing tunes together and presenting them. That whole concept thing, and the control and delivery that went into it, was pretty inspiring to me.

I don't know if Ian Anderson was a control freak, I wasn't in his band. But I do know he worked his ass off to control his environment to the point of making sure that everything, right down to the lights, were set up. They were actually very soft artistic people. Martin Barre, the guitar player, was especially that way. Being that he was kind of small and I was so tall that it made him seem even more shy. But obviously Ian was the power guy. They were all clean living, successful and real different from the typical Led Zeppelin types - you know the "dick, balls, tits and whisky" type of guys. It wasn't that putrid rock crap.

Ian's involvement with Mallard was based more on a friendship level than anything else. It wasn't a business deal - I mean I doubt he thought he was going to be making a bunch of money out of Mallard. It was a tax write off I'm sure. When I went down to talk to him, he was staying at the Beverly Hilton, and there's me living in some trailer in the middle of the desert. So, we get into his limo and drive to this very spiffy Beverly Hills restaurant, and it's just me and Ian! So there I am sitting in these tattered clothes while four waiters are bringing us lobster and this bitchin' wine. Quite a dining experience to have four people fawn over you. I don't know what that dinner cost, but man it was the dinner of my lifetime!

With Mallard we decided not to gig or tour at that time. The idea was to try and put an album together in order to get a record deal. We started by putting the tunes together without Artie - he was back selling insurance in Pittsburg. John French had also gone. So it was really just Mark and me. We brought back Art when we flew over to England to do the album. Sam Galpin also joined just before we left. I auditioned a lot of singers, most of whom were guys in leather pants with attitudes. Sam was obviously from a different place - his leg was in a cast when I first met him. He had been a country singer in Vegas and you could hear that in his voice. He must have thought, "I'll follow these guys over to England to do a record. At least it's a paycheck."

The recording sessions for the first Mallard album were done at Martin Barre's house in England. He was gracious enough to let us stay in the small house - which was still bigger than the house I'm living in now! We set up a mobile unit in his barn, it was a good situation. So we recorded the basic tracks and did whatever minimal overdubs were necessary there. The studio was basically for sequencing. But the main sessions were done in the barn and recorded on Ian Anderson's big mobile truck which was parked outside.

CHAPTER TWENTY-FOUR
Back On The Pavement

"Back On The Pavement" was definitely built off of a blues-based feel. I had reconnected with a friend of mine, David Wagstaff, a guy I'd gone to highschool and hung around with - in fact he lives near me now. He was a good writer and I just wrote the music to these words that he had written about Vietnam.

The feel of "She's Long And She's Lean" came from a riff Mark had been playing. I should credit Mark Boston a lot more for his effort on the material than I did at the time - which I do feel bad about. His roots were very country, but what I was into playing was a lot jazzier than that. Musically I felt strained. So I put my strain back onto him.

Ted Alvy, another friend of mine that I had met in Northern California in 1972, also wrote some lyrics. With Ted he didn't have things already existing, so I would go to him with some sounds and describe things that I needed from the vocal phrases. I didn't write lyrics really.

Mark and I were given credit for writing "Road To Morrocco". It was almost done in the manner of the earlier Beefheart stuff where we chiseled away at it. It was hard to get Artie to free-form solo, so the marimba solo came about while we were practising and then I said, "that's a take!"

"One Day Once" was a tune we were playing when the band was still called the Magic Band. John wrote the lyrics and I was given credit for the music. But this song was actually based on one of Mark Marcellino's keyboard riffs so his name should have been on that tune.

"Yellow" was my first endeavour into playing a nylon string guitar. I was at the point where I was teaching myself how to read music and beginning to play some classical pieces. So this was, to my ear, pleasing little sounds that I made on a classical guitar.

"Desperados Waiting For A Train" was a cool country-based tune that we worked on to bring Sam into the sound. "A Piece Of Me" was me and John French - John doing the lyrics and me doing the musical parts. Again that came from the beginning of the Magic Band as a separate unit. John was just basically the vocalist at that time with Art on the "tubs" as he called them.

"Reign Of Pain" was an older song that John had played when he was in a group called Rattlesnakes & Eggs and I was still in the Beefheart band. It was so John French I couldn't believe it. It had some cool parts to it the way they intertwined and things. I didn't know Dan Moore who wrote the lyrics - he was somebody John knew. I liked the tune from a musical standpoint - it was funny. Actually as John told me later, we had turned the parts around and played it wrong. But that's how we played it and that's how it came out.

"South Of The Valley" was another John French tune where they gave me an arrangement credit. But it was John's tune, pretty obvious little ditty - couple of chords back and forth. Maybe I was being a hog, or maybe Bill Shumow the manager was trying to put me in control - I don't know. But my name showed up a little too often on occasions, even though I did pretty much control the arrangements to everything.

"Winged Tuskadero" was actually the tune that was originally called "Mallard Ballad". If you listen to it, it is early swing hip hop. It was David's lyrics and me putting the parts together. I kind of liked it.

The reason we re-did the old Beefheart tune "Peon" - at least my reasoning - is that it was done for the people who would come up to me and say, "Oh, we liked what you used to play", the edginess of it and all that. I just wanted to make it more musical. So in that process I'm sure I pissed off a lot of people, just because it didn't sound like it used to anymore. It sounded like a guitar instead of tortured metal. It was also a very conscious thing for me to try to bury my past with the Beefheart band. The way we recorded it at Martin's house with that very sleepy feel with the birds outside and everything, it was very distant, almost vaporizing. My idea was to bury that feeling of grief - it felt appropriate.

There was no way Mallard was supposed to be competing with the Beefheart band. Because the imagery that Don projected through his lyrics, it was never going to come across in that way, no matter how musically 'out there' we were. I wasn't even worried about the comparisons. I figured for every fan we dropped we might gain one. But didn't pay attention to the critics' response a whole lot. Some people thought, "oh yeh there are some elements that are kind of cool, almost Beefheartish". But we didn't really have fans as such - we'd only played a couple of gigs.

Still, I think it was a little bit overwhelming because I was still carrying so much weight from previously being in the Beefheart band. I was having mixed feelings about the music business in general. Obviously, I was trying to make a living, but at the same time I was having feelings of, "I don't even want to do this, I just want to camp out and practise guitar and not have to deal with the tensions of the music business."

So that's what the first Mallard album was about. A lot of people say that they definitely prefer this one to the second one. I'm completely the opposite. Again anything I listen to from this long ago is just nauseating because it's so weak. But the thing people tell me they like is the rawness or "the realness" of the first one as opposed to the slickness of the second. I'm still in disagreement with that.

What I do know is that the first Mallard LP was definitely better than *Unconditionally Guaranteed.* It got a little bit gooey in a lot of places for me. There were some real sappy, embarrassing parts to me - but there always are. I still say it didn't sound like standard issue pop music - you know, "Here's the little ditty and look here comes the hook!" But some of the elements might have improved if they had been played over and over again.

Probably my big failing is that once I do something I don't stick at it - I go somewhere else. So I'm kind of a "greenhorn" at whatever I'm doing. But that's just what feels natural to me instead of becoming a blues player and playing Stevie Ray Vaughan licks over and over. I just can't do that, it's incredibly boring to me and lacks creativity - but you sure can become proficient at it. I can admire the sound when I hear it but I couldn't live that process - becoming a great guitarist that plays five notes better than somebody else.

CHAPTER TWENTY-FIVE
Life In A Different Climate

Again, *In A Different Climate* was recorded on Ian Anderson's mobile unit - I believe he was actually paid for it this time, so it wasn't just a loan job. Not that he was doing it for the money obviously. But we did it at a place called Clearwell Castle in Wales. They pulled in this recording unit in a big Mercedes truck and ran cables down into the basement of the castle. The accommodation was top notch - it was a nice environment.

Art Tripp didn't really quit the band because he wasn't ever really in it. But by this time he just didn't want any part of it anymore - I can't blame him. If there had been some money - a reason for him to keep going through the grief - he probably would have stayed. But he went back to selling insurance.

Well being as nice as I can to George Dragota - I must say my strengths are not in picking musicians - he was a very nice guy and he had played drums with some LA bands. He was real upbeat and easy to work with, and that was the attractive part of it. As far as his style meshing with ours - it didn't quite work out. We needed somebody who was very heavy. I'm sure the sessions were very difficult for him, but I must say he held it together on an emotional level very well. I probably was a 'brute' - you know, "Come on, hit it harder - do this, do that!" But that was my mistake, we should have picked a heavier handed drummer.

Our main concern at the time was "get the album done!" But when we went over to England, all of a sudden we found out we've got six gigs lined up - one at the Reading Festival, The Rainbow in London and whatever. Clover, who later became Huey Lewis and The News was the opening act. We were totally unprepared for these gigs. We thought we were just doing the recording sessions, all of a sudden we had to create a show from two albums' worth of material. Basically, we played everything on these albums with the exception of a couple of tunes. And actually they came out OK - I've heard some bootlegs of it and it sounds pretty nervous but 'all right'.

The basic theme of "Green Coyote" came from a guitar riff of Mark's, and the rest kind of came from me re-working it. The tune was written around the lyrics by David Wagstaff. Actually I like the tune - it had that sense of cartoonishness about it. I just thought it came off well.

"Your Face On Someone Else" was another Wagstaff lyric, and that's when John Thomas entered the picture. He was a very young guy at that time, and a very good keyboard player. He was also a big time Zappa/Beefheart fan, and he could play the "Battle Hymn Of The Republic" like nobody else. He was a quirky person, one of 13 children. Now I think he's playing with Bruce Hornsby's band, and he's worked with Don Henley and various acts. His keyboard work in the process of recording this album really helped to solidify parts. Even so, he was one of the people that liked the first album better. I don't know, maybe because he saw the process on the second album. Anyway "Your Face On Someone Else" is that thing of delving into a jazzier sound.

"Harvest" was another country tune based around Sam Galpin. John Thomas wrote the music, but this was definitely way too 'Eagles' for me. But I wasn't gonna control things to the point where I said, "No, we're not gonna play this country crap". So I wasn't real happy about it, but I thought it was a good tune for what it was. I don't think our rendition of it was very good.

"Mama Squeeze" was right up my alley, again getting into a swing funk thing. I gave Ted some lyrical ideas and I liked the tune. John's moog synthesizer parts were actually sampled for use on KHJ TV in LA for a while.

"Heartstrings" was a grandiose thing that better players should have played. But the tune was one of those long tunes - an epic or whatever. "Old Man Grey" was all Mark, while "Texas Weather" is a 'push beat boogie woogie' thing. I remember thinking I just wanted to play something in that groove - my girlfriend was from Texas at the time. The song could have been OK but it's a little stilted.

I have mixed feelings about "Big Foot". It was a tune that might have been my favorite from the album except it got clever with the overdubs. Some good elements in there that I liked - time changes, slow swing. It sounds like it could have been on *Clear Spot*, with a different groove and different production and stuff. So on that album, "Green Coyote", "Mama Squeeze" and "Big Foot" were the three that stood out for me. I'm sure everybody else disagrees with me and they think "Old Man Grey" is the best thing on the album. All I know is that the album reached the Billboard charts. So there was more reaction to it than the previous one, maybe it was partly due to availability.

While the first Mallard album had been recorded in just a few days, the second took some time to work all the parts in. By the time it got to my overdubbed solo parts, it just happened to be one of those days when I couldn't play. So it's tough for me to live with a lot the guitar parts on the second album. Because I had written things that were at the very edge of my ability, when it came to doing it I couldn't play for shit. And Simon, who I think was the vice president at Virgin underneath Richard Branson, was sitting in the studio looking at his watch and I'm playing like shit! Time is ticking by and the band's gone, I'm the only person left there and I'm doing these guitar parts and I'm totally coming unglued!

Mallard broke up from a mixture of internal differences, financial problems and record company non-support. We were set to do a tour, and Virgin Records was only Europe at the time. The American distributorship was WEA or CBS. I think they changed from WEA to CBS. Well in that process the new US distributor decided to drop the album. And the tour money, the way the story was told to me, ended up in some guy's pocket who left the company - never to be found again.

If the tour thing had happened, for once we would have had a little bit of money. Well that's not strictly true, we actually got some money upfront after we signed for the second Mallard album. So there was some money, and that was distributed through all the band. We lived on that for a while, but it didn't last long.

In the mean time I had done some music for an hour long film for a friend of mine's masters project - music that was really different. That was fun and it really got me going on the idea of coming up with just small bits of sound to match film. After that, the idea of going back to 'being in a band' - I just couldn't do it anymore.

I did think about keeping it going, I even talked to another bass player. I feel pretty bad about that because Mark had been such an integral part of the band. But I just needed somebody that was moving more towards the fusion things I was doing, or trying to do anyway.

CHAPTER TWENTY-SIX
I'm Out Of Here

After the band broke up, my girlfriend at the time was a bilingual education teacher and we had the choice between moving to Oregon or Caracas, Venezuela. We chose Oregon, which I think that was the right decision, so that's where we ended up. I was done with Mallard. I'd made the decision "I'm out of here", and I felt pretty comfortable with that.

It was harder to feel comfortable with the way we were treated by the record company. The story goes that we signed 'an intent to sign' so we could go ahead and record the second album. When the complete contract was ready for signing it had, shall we say, a major problem. I won't go into details, but I don't remember signing the contract they currently hold.

The result was that I made no money on those albums. They say I still owe them like £36,000 pounds or something. Then when the albums came out together on the one CD, they contacted me and offered me half the going rate to write my own liner notes.

Then, they wrote me a note and said I had unduly delayed the process of the release of the album, because in part of the contract it said the second album was solely mine for American release. Well since I apparently delayed it, they got somebody else to write the liner notes. Finally I just went, "forget it, yeh they owe me money. But what will it take to get it?" I'm solvent enough now not to worry about a few grand.

As regards to what the other members of Mallard did after the break-up. Sam Galpin, I don't know what he did. Art Tripp was already in Pittsburg selling insurance. Later he went back to LA and got into the music business and did some studio work, including working on Captain Beefheart's *Shiny Beast* album. Then after that he became a chiropractor, which he's currently still doing.

Mark bounced around in various bands. I ran into him about 7 years later, after I had moved to Oregon. He was playing in a covers type band. I was doing much the same in Oregon, I played three nights a week in a country band playing bass. It doesn't sound very glorified, but it was positive for me to just get away and be able to support myself and actually pay rent. It was a scary environment but it was easy money, and the people I was playing with were very nice people. Country music wasn't my forte of course, but for three nights a week I was making good money.

Then I started teaching during the day about 3 or 4 days a week. That's when I really got geared up and was practising 6 hours a day, and started to learn classical guitar. I also taught myself how to read and get into the math-theory of music.

Way after this, around 1990 Henry Kaiser threw me a bone and I did one cut on the *Slide Crazy* album (various artists album of slide guitar work on Rykodisc). I also worked on John French's album. He sent me a disk of the parts so I could just boot it up and midi up the parts, and then play to that. What I did was play directly to a DAT tape, and they dubbed that onto the music. But some of the parts were changed from those I had played to, so I sounded rhythmically kinda foolish in places. It made me sound like I was making mistakes that I didn't make.

Then I started to get this onslaught of phone calls - people contacting me just kind of out of nowhere after years and years. I think it may be the internet, or maybe old fans had reached age of finally being old enough to start re-looking up people that were important to them. But anyway I got a lot of offers just all of a sudden. One was from Bubblehead Music and they were very professional, and very nice. I did four tunes for them, and I was under the impression that it was going to be a film project - in fact they turned it into an album. They just sent me the ADAT tapes with their stuff, and they give me no parameters - "just play!"

Then, this guy Ant-Bee (Billy James) called, he lives near golf country, and I played an acoustic guitar piece for him for his fourth album *Electronic Church Muzik*. He wanted a traditional old delta blues style tune with a Zoot Horn Rollo signature in the middle of it. Jimmy Carl Black - the Indian of the group - did the voice over to it. It was then manipulated by Patrick Ogelvie at Flux Audio in Wilmington, NC to sound like an old scratchy 78 record from the 30's.

CHAPTER TWENTY-SEVEN
I Am Zoot Horn Rollo

I have been teaching guitar for the past 20 years - constantly playing and teaching has been my main interest - I really enjoy it!!! But I haven't played in front of an audience in 10 years - I don't miss it. I miss playing with people - but not in front of people.

I love teaching, sometimes like anything it's very hard, but it's a way for me to connect with people. Teaching is befriending and passing on a little bit of information, rather than telling people what you know or how your version of 'life as a musician' is. It's about getting their trust. Fortunately I'm in a small enough place where I'm a moderately sized fish in a very small pond. So I have been able to have a full slate of students for quite a while now.

Very few of my students know my musical background at the beginning. Some find out and look at me strange. Others find out and it can get in the way. Other people did know and it wasn't a problem. They were grown-ups, and they were very professional about the student/teacher situation. But usually I try to keep it a secret, and the main reason is that if they are Zoot Horn Rollo fans, that usually means *Trout Mask Replica* fans, and they aren't getting any of that from me now! That was a thousand years ago. I don't know any of those parts now, and I don't play like that - I don't aspire to play like that. I'm not going to show somebody else how to play a memorized part like that - there's no reason for it.

I get lots of requests for transcriptions of guitar parts - as if I'm likely to remember! I usually say, "Ask Henry Kaiser, he knows more about my guitar parts than I do at this point in time". He took all the tapes, separated all the parts and learned most of them. An incredible feat! Jesus!

Occasionally I will use my background if I get a young guitar student that's got 'attitude' stuff, and it's one of those, "Show me man, prove to me..." Then when they figure out that, "Oh you've made albums, and you've toured and done this..." Then all of a sudden there's this credibility thing and I can use it as a lever to get across to some of the puberty-laden youths.

I'm currently working on a teaching tool. I noticed after teaching for 20 years, that I kept having all these circles on the floor, of the way I would relate chords together. It's about modes and what I call context. So I'm working on an invention - the 'Rollo Mode Wheel'.

The last time I saw Don was in Lancaster in the desert. I think the Mallard stuff had happened and was over. He didn't seem particularly happy. It was a real interesting reaction because I had expected this "Oh you're an asshole, you left me" kinda thing. And yet he was kind of fawning all over me. I'll leave it at that. It was kind of this casual thing. I saw him that evening and that was the last time.

Actually it would be nice to talk to him again. I miss the person - but if I was to call him I would be on the phone for the rest of my life talking to him. That was why through the years I haven't talked to him because once he'd get my phone number I would be on the phone everyday with him. I understand he's not healthy and I certainly wish him the best. I'd like to talk to the man but he never made it easy. If there was a way I could have contact with him, and make it an easy situation, I would do it in a minute. He is a very powerful, interesting person.

As regards to the albums he made after the band broke up, *Blue-jeans and Moonbeams* I heard once and can't remember it. I haven't heard much of *Shiny Beast, Doc At The Radar Station* and *Ice Cream For Crow*. I heard the one song "Ice Cream For Crow" that appeared on a video that somebody sent me of a bunch of Beefheart stuff. As I remember it, it was very reminiscent of the early days. But then some of the tunes were around back when I was in the band. And when I heard people saying that they were good, I didn't even care. I was there the first time, like I need to hear it again. I'd moved on!

I'm glad he became successful as a painter, that's where I think one of his large talents lie. I don't know him today. I don't know if he's the same. I've seen some interviews, like the *Letterman Show*, where he acted strange but I think that was just an act. I mean I hung around with the guy long enough to tell. You know, he'd come out of the bathroom and talk like a normal guy. But I think he faked it until he became it, and he seemed to be really out of touch in certain ways. Although I'm sure he was aware how the *Letterman Show* would affect people's view of him, he seemed a bit lost.

As regards to the other ex-Magic Band members. John French, I just saw recently. So we have stayed in touch. Mark, I haven't talked to in a while. The last time I talked to him he called me from North Carolina, I think. It didn't sound like he was in a great situation. Not horrible, he wasn't in jail or anything, but it didn't sound like he was happy with his life. He was talking about coming out here for the music scene, and I said, "What music scene?" Art Tripp, I've kept in touch with, he lives in Northern California just south of me. He seems very fine and happy.

Recently Bill Shumow called me. One of his sons was learning "I'm Gonna Booglarize You Baby", so we took the opportunity to shoot the breeze. Then I heard he was ill, I called him at the hospital and we had a long conversation. Then the next thing I heard was that he had passed away. I couldn't believe it, he was such an important person to me and spanned the entire time I was in the band. He was a good friend and more specifically he didn't put up with the bullshit in the

Beefheart band. Or perhaps even more to the point, he didn't feed it. He was a good stable person for me to hang around.

I also enjoy playing golf. I always enjoyed a lot of sports, I was way into baseball when I was a kid. As I have gotten older, I suffer from Labrynthitis constantly, which is a middle ear problem where I walk like I'm on a boat, so I look like I'm drunk when I'm not. So with golf it was a ball that just sat on the ground, and I could hit it. Being tall and skinny I was always a finesse athlete rather than a power type. So golf fit in with my mentality. At the ripe old age of 48, as I write this, I'm still able to get better. My handicap is 3 right now, and that's tough to do when I only play once a week.

I still listen to quite a lot of music these days, because managing a music store I hear a lot of everything. And the good part of that has been that I've kept current with things, even things that I would have gone, "That's a bunch of shit, this rap shit!" Actually it keeps me in touch and has been healthy for me.

I don't really have any favorite musical artists, there's certain people that I respect. I'd probably have to say Michael Brecker, and the reason is because here's a guy with tremendous chops that connect to the 'Coltrane' past. He plays everything from Joni Mitchell pop stuff to hard core jazz. He uses newer Midi instruments and very straight sounding instruments, and he mixes them all together very well. There's very few people I can imagine who can play so dynamically in varied situations.

Pat Metheny's a great guitar player, and I really enjoy his playing because his voice is so identifiable. He seems determined to prove he can play anything. But I still don't hear anybody with the breadth that Brecker has. Ralph Towner is a favorite guitar player of mine. I really like his writing, his playing and his economy of notes. These are very intelligent people that have dedicated their lives to music.

I guess the best live thing I've seen recently was Jan Garbarek. It was gorgeous, organic breathing stuff - very simple and melodic. No it's not straight ahead jazz, I think a lot of it was based on Norwegian folk melodies - gorgeous playing!

As I said before, the real difference between the old days and now is you know exactly how you're getting screwed. It's big business and they couldn't give a shit about you. It's obvious from the retail end that they don't care about the people who buy and sell their records/cds. It's just this enormously marked up profit margin for the 'fat cats', and it's always been that way. And if you go into it thinking anything else, it's your fault not theirs.

The whole idea of something like 'paying to play a gig' is absurd. It's just a tough business and everybody pays now. When I started, shit nobody paid! God, if you could stand up straight and tune your guitar, you had a contract.

It seems really defined now, people can have a niche and support themselves in the music business in smaller ways, which scares the shit out of the big companies. But in general, there's a lot of good stuff that's never going to be mainstream, and never has been. There have been accidental periods when it's happened, the 60's was one. For me the late 70's, when the fusion stuff was very strong from the Miles Davis influence - Weather Report and so forth - was another. Imagine Weather Report selling out a concert, I mean it blows my mind! But in general, the big bands that sell are the Hootie & the Blowfish's of this world. It's always been about the lowest common denominator. I can't imagine how it could ever be anything else but.

I guess it's a real compliment to be quoted as an influential band - mostly due to Don of course. I always knew that it was Don that they were talking about - and it should be. No question about that. He was the main influence. But there have been instances when people have let me know that my guitar playing was influential and that's a great compliment too. I guess I could put it the other way around. I can remember exactly what I was doing when I first heard a particular Beatles song. I can remember which girl I was trying to go out with, the smell of her sweater, that sort of thing! God knows what these people envision when they hear a Beefheart song!

I have some very good musician friends, the Bosworth family, three brothers who grew up listening to Beefheart and through them I heard some great stories of how they reacted to that. For example, one of them had read in an interview that we had played wearing lampshades on our heads - so they tried to do that. They were only 13 or so at the time, young enough to do something silly like that.

I know that people from Devo to Johnny Rotten have quoted us as influential. The British side was really strong, probably because we were very successful there, although I haven't really kept up with that. I know that different acts have covered our songs, many of them British. I'm glad that people even now can get something really positive from it. It's simply a great compliment.

Other than those people who were directly influenced by us, I can see that some bands have a similar spirit. Managing a CD store I get to listen to a great deal of music that I definitely wouldn't choose to listen to. Sometimes I hear something that has the same spirit and ethic that we had. They probably don't want to get too close to our true spirit because this is not the late sixties or early seventies, where there was some money available to anyone who could stand up there and play. Current bands need to sell CDs to survive. There's just a glut of bands, there's way too much music out there at the moment, most of it bad. To suss out where these little nuggets are is an incredibly difficult process compared to people discovering Beefheart when there were maybe only 20 bands that might fall into that category. That's a lot easier than the 10,000 bands you might have to ferret through these days.

As I said, there are a lot of bands who have creative elements that, as I listen to them now, come from that spirit. "We don't know shit about music, we know a few notes and we are going to get as experimental as hell with them!" That is a big part of the spirit of the Magic Band. No matter who knew how to read music, who knew music theory - Artie being one who did, me being one who did not - we only used any music theory to communicate an idea. It was totally driven by a sense of rhythm, propulsion, shape and texture. Even the very simplest parts of *Clear Spot* came with that mentality.

In hindsight I don't have any regrets - I am Zoot Horn Rollo. I learned a lot. It sure wasn't a 'walk in the park'. It's hard to think of it as a career. I surely didn't treat it as one. That was just what I did, and it was a kind of like an elongated period of adolescence. As I look at my contemporaries who still continue to be involved in the music business, most are probably quite well off - the one's that didn't kill themselves with drugs. I guess if I had a regret, it would be that I didn't have an adult enough attitude in my 20's to carry on, and realize that I could have been more successful than I am now. I got into music for music rather than trying to make a living out of it. I only grew up after that. But I'm quite comfortable and happy now. 35 hours at a store, teach 30 students, keep my golf game together, practice guitar - I'm very happily married and I have a dog and cat - you know.

COMING SOON FROM SAF PUBLISHING AND FIREFLY PUBLISHING

GO AHEAD JOHN - The Music Of John McLaughlin by Paul Stump - SAF Publishing

ISBN 0946719 24 1   **192 pages (illustrated)**   **UK Price £12.99**

John McLaughlin is one of the premier jazz guitarists of modern times. Over a long and varied career spanning three decades, he was initially nurtured by Miles Davis and played on such seminal LPs as *Bitches Brew* and *Jack Johnson*. In the 70s he formed the Mahavishnu Orchestra, a group that forged a new link between rock and jazz. Subsequently he has created fusions with Indian and Spanish music, and has collaborated with such varied musicians as Carlos Santana, Paco de Lucia, Al DiMeola and Trilok Gurtu. Filling concert halls the world over, McLaughlin remains a guitarist of dazzling speed and invention, one of the most respected jazz musicians of his age. Paul Stump fascinatingly assesses McLaughlin's huge contribution to both Rock and Jazz as well casting a critical eye over his recorded output.

PROCOL HARUM - Beyond The Pale by Claes Johansen - SAF Publishing

ISBN 0946719 28 4   **192 pages (illustrated)**   **UK Price £12.99**

In May 1967 a totally unknown and strangely named group smashed into the charts all over the world with an innovative and overpowering sound. The song was called "A Whiter Shade Of Pale", the group Procol Harum. Combining Gary Brooker's soulful voice, Keith Reid's enigmatic lyrics and Matthew Fisher's sweeping organ it became one of the enduring anthems of the 60s and stayed at number one for six weeks in the UK. Over the next ten years Procol Harum continued to produce some of the best records of the era, including all-time classic albums such as *Shine On Brightly, A Salty Dog* and *Broken Barricades*. They broke up in 1977, only to reform with much acclaim in 1991 with a line-up including original members Gary Brooker, Keith Reid, Matthew Fisher and Robin Trower. Novelist and musician Claes Johansen has spent many years researching the group's history - *Beyond The Pale* is a profound and insightful look at one of Britain's finest ever rock acts.

SOUL SACRIFICE - A History of Santana by Simon Leng - Firefly Publishing

ISBN 0946719 29 2   **192 pages (illustrated)**   **UK Price £12.99**

Led by the Mexican-born guitarist of the same name, Santana came to prominence at the Woodstock festival of 1969. Genuinely the first band to incorporate Latin rhythms fully into rock, Santana's music has always been dominated by the fluid guitar playing of their leader. Still regularly recording and touring, Santana has recently worked with John Lee Hooker. This is the first full biography of the band and the pioneering spirit of their leader.

GINGER GEEZER - Viv Stanshall & the Bonzo Dog Band by Chris Welch & Lucian Randall - SAF Publishing

ISBN: 09467119 27 6   **224 pages (illustrated)**   **UK Price £12.99**

Viv Stanshall was one of pop music's true originals. During the sixties he fronted one of Britain's funniest and most surreal musical outfits, The Bonzo Dog Doo Dah Band. However, Stanshall's life was one of extreme highs and lows, varying from playing pranks with The Who's Keith Moon to depression, alcoholism, and his final sad demise in a house fire. Former Melody Maker editor Chris Welch is a long-time Stanshall afficianado and recounts his incredible life story - a man who on the one hand could write lyrics for Steve Winwood, whilst on the other accused of attempting to murder his wife.

OPENING THE MUSICAL BOX: A Genesis Chronicle by Alan Hewitt - Firefly

ISBN: 0946 719 30 6   **200 pages (illustrated)**   **UK Price: £12.99**

Compiled by the editor of The Waiting Room, the definitive Genesis Magazine, Opening The Musical Box is the bible for all things Genesis. Featuring interviews with all members and ex-members it traces the band from their beginnings at Charterhouse school through to worldwide international stardom.

Genesis have gone through many incarnations. As pioneers of progressive rock, mini opuses such as "Supper's Ready" and "Tale of the Giant Hogweed", made them one of the most popular live acts of the early seventies. With Peter Gabriel's theatrical eye for presentation, the early band peaked with what many consider an under-rated masterpiece The Lamb Lies Down On Broadway.

After Gabriel's departure, drummer Phil Collins took over the helm of the band and the rest is history, as they say. After numerous hit LPs and millions of record sales, Collins himself departed to leave Mike Rutherford and Tony Banks to forge forward with the band's career.

This highly detailed and informative analysis of the band's music follows over 30 years of musical activity. Featuring a complete discography and gigography, never before have all the facts and figures about this highly inventive band been collected together in one place. A must for devotees and new fans alike.

Also coming soon:

Manic Street Preachers by Ben Roberts (Firefly)

Available Now:

AN AMERICAN BAND - The Story of Grand Funk Railroad by Billy James - SAF Publishing

ISBN: 09467119 26 8	192 pages (illustrated)	UK Price £12.99

"The book chronologically lays out the boys' story, with handy subheadings introducing new characters and scenes, sketched with clarity and bolstered by many critical reviews. If you want a clear, well-written account about one of the oft-forgotten pioneers of hard rock, then this is a safe and satisfying bet." **Record Collector**

"Biographer Billy James managed to interview all band members and makes no bones about where his loyalties lay. To be honest, his pro Funk enthusiasm makes for a compelling read. There are some great anecdotes. James honestly explores the band's split with Knight and how Grand Funk managed to maintain momentum without his tireless publicising." **Record Mart & Buyer**

"The author's belligerence shines through: this is his long-fermented diatribe against the dons of rock crit - the Marcuses and Christgaus - who mocked his favourite band. In that, like Grand Funk Railroad themselves, it has a certain charm." **Q Magazine**

Wish The World Away - Mark Eitzel and the American Music Club by Sean Body

ISBN: 0 946719 20 9	192 pages (illustrated)	UK Price £12.99

An insightful, analytical, warts-and-all portrait of what makes a great writer of "pretentious little songs of quiet self-loathing". Eitzel's words naturally. **Mojo**

Wish The World Away is an insightful, quote-drenched post-mortem on a band who recorded a slew of unbearably moving records before getting chewed up by the music biz machine. **Uncut**

LUNAR NOTES - Zoot Horn Rollo's Captain Beefheart Experience by Bill Harkleroad with Billy James

ISBN: 0 946719 217	160 pages (illustrated) -	UK Price £11.95

Bill Harkleroad joined Captain Beefheart's Magic Band at a crucial time in their development. Beefheart rechristened Harkleroad as Zoot Horn Rollo and they embarked on recording one of the classic rock albums of all time - Trout Mask Replica - a work of unequalled daring and inventiveness. Further LPs, Lick My Decals Off Baby and Clear Spot, highlighted Zoot's skilled guitar playing and what a truly innovative band they were. For the first time we get the insider's story of what it was like to record, play and live with an eccentric genius such as Beefheart.

MEET THE RESIDENTS - America's Most Eccentric Band! by Ian Shirley

ISBN: 0946 719 12 8   **200 pages (illustrated)**   **UK Price £11.95**

Fully updated and now available again! An outsider's view of The Residents' operations, exposing a world where nothing is as it seems. It is a fascinating tale of the musical anarchy and cartoon wackiness that has driven this unique bunch of artistic mavericks forward.

"This is the nearest to an official history you are ever likely to get, slyly abetted by the bug-eyed beans from Venus themselves". **Vox**   *"Few enthusiasts will want to put this book down once they start reading".* **Record Collector**

DIGITAL GOTHIC - A Critical Discography Of Tangerine Dream by Paul Stump

ISBN: 0946 719 18 7   **160 pages (illustrated)**   **UK Price £9.95**

In this critical discography, music journalist Paul Stump picks his way through a veritable minefield of releases, determining both the explosive and those which fail to ignite. For the very first time Tangerine Dream's mammoth output is placed within an ordered perspective.

"It focuses fascinatingly on the pre-soporific roots of the group and their place in a cool electronic lineage which traces right up to Detroit techno". **Mojo**   *"A stimulating companion to the group's music".* **The Wire**

THE ONE AND ONLY : Peter Perrett - Homme Fatale by Nina Antonia

ISBN: 0946 719 16 0   **224 pages (illustrated).**   **UK Price £11.95**

An extraordinary journey through crime, punishment and the decadent times of The Only Ones. Includes interviews with Perrett and all ex-band members.

"Antonia gets everyone's co-operation and never loses her perspective on Perrett". **Mojo**

"Antonia is the ideal chronicler of Perrett's rise and fall. From his time as drug dealer, to the smack sojourn in The Only Ones, Perrett's tale is one of self-abuse and staggering selfishness". **Select**

Plunderphonics, 'Pataphysics and Pop Mechanics by Andrew Jones

ISBN: 0946 719 15 2   **256 pages (illustrated)**   **UK Price £12.95**

Chris Cutler, Fred Frith, Henry Threadgill, Ferdinand Richard, Amy Denio, Lindsay Cooper, John Oswald, John Zorn, The Residents and many more...

"The talent assembled between Jones's covers would be interesting under any rubric. Thought provoking and stimulating". **Mojo**   *"Jones's book is perhaps the first study of the growth of these techniques within the avant-garde. Packed with fascinating interviews and written with wit and insight".* **Q magazine**

KRAFTWERK - Man, Machine and Music by Pascal Bussy

ISBN: 0946 719 09 8   **200 pages (illustrated).**   **UK Price £11.95**

Uniquely definitive account of Kraftwerk's history, delving beyond their publicity shunning exterior to reveal the full story behind one of the most influential bands in the history of rock music. Based on interviews with Ralf Hutter, Florian Schneider, Karl Bartos, Emil Schult and many more.

"Bussy engagingly explains why they are one of the few groups who've actually changed how music sounds". **Q magazine.**   *"I doubt this book will ever be bettered".* **Vox**

Wrong Movements - A Robert Wyatt History by Mike King

ISBN: 0946 719 10 1   **160 pages (illustrated).**   **UK Price £14.95**

A sumptuous and detailed journey through Robert Wyatt's 30 year career with Soft Machine, Matching Mole and as a highly respected solo artist. Packed with previously unpublished archive material and rare photos. Commentary from Wyatt himself, Hugh Hopper, Mike Ratledge, Daevid Allen, Kevin Ayers & more.

"King's careful chronology and Wyatt's supreme modesty produce a marvellously unhysterical, oddly haunting book". **Q magazine**   *"Low key, likeable and lefty. Like the man himself".* **iD magazine**

No More Mr. Nice Guy - The Inside Story of the Alice Cooper Group by Michael Bruce & Billy James

ISBN: 0946 719 17 9   160 pages (illustrated).   UK Price £9.95

Original guitarist and songwriter Michael Bruce opens the lid on his years with the platinum selling group, revealing the truth behind the publicity stunts, the dead babies, the drinking, the executions and, of course, the rock 'n' roll.

"I'm Eighteen changed Alice Cooper from the group that destroyed chickens to the group that destroyed stadiums".
Village Voice.

"It might even be argued that the band defined what it meant to be a role ridden seventies teenager". **Rolling Stone**

WIRE - Everybody Loves a History by Kevin Eden

ISBN: 0946 719 07 1   192 pages (illustrated).   UK Price £9.95

A fascinating look at one of punk's most endearing and enduring bands, including interviews with all band members. A self-analysis of the complex motivations which have often seen the various members cross the boundaries between music and art.

"Any band or their fans could feel well served by a book like Eden's". **Vox**

"Eden delivers a sharp portrayal of the punk industry's behaviour, influence and morality". **Q magazine**

TAPE DELAY by Charles Neal

ISBN: 0946 719 02 0   256 pages (illustrated).   UK Price £11.95

Marc Almond, Cabaret Voltaire, Nick Cave, Chris & Cosey, Coil, Foetus, Neubauten, Non, The Fall, The The, Lydia Lunch, New Order, Psychic TV, Rollins, Sonic Youth, Swans, Test Department and many more...

"A virtual Who's Who of people who've done the most to drag music out of commercial confinement". **NME**

"Intriguing and interesting". **Q magazine**

Dark Entries - Bauhaus and Beyond by Ian Shirley

ISBN: 0946 719 13 6   200 pages (illustrated).   UK Price £11.95

The full gothic rise and fall of Bauhaus, including offshoot projects Love and Rockets, Tones on Tail, Daniel Ash, David J and Peter Murphy. Ian Shirley unravels the uncompromising story of four individuals who have consistently confounded their detractors by turning up the unexpected.

"A brilliant trench-to-toilet missive of who did what, where and when. It works brilliantly". **Alternative Press**

"Solidly researched account of goth-tinged glam". **Top Magazine**

M7031-TX
39